Ancient Peoples ...

WRITING

General Editor

DR. GLYN DANIEL

Ancient Peoples and Places

WRITING

David Diringer

78 PHOTOGRAPHS
49 LINE DRAWINGS
AND 3 MAPS

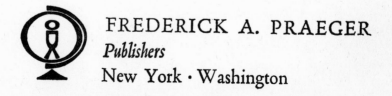

FREDERICK A. PRAEGER
Publishers
New York · Washington

♥

THIS IS VOLUME TWENTY-FIVE IN THE SERIES
Ancient Peoples and Places
GENERAL EDITOR: DR. GLYN DANIEL

BOOKS THAT MATTER *Published in the United States of America*
in 1962 by Frederick A. Praeger, Inc.
Publisher, 111 Fourth Avenue
New York 3, N.Y.
Second printing, 1965
All rights reserved
Library of Congress Catalog Card Number: 62-8211
© David Diringer 1962
Printed in Holland by Koninklijke Drukkerij
G. J. Thieme N.V., Nijmegen

411
D

CONTENTS

332425

ILLUSTRATIONS

8

General Editor's Foreword

When this series of books was first planned it was intended that each volume should describe an ancient people or a place where peoples lived in antiquity. As the series has developed it has been decided to modify this initial purpose: we published in 1960 Bosi's book on *The Lapps* which dealt with a living people, but people who preserved to the present day an ancient way of life; and now we publish a book dealing with neither an ancient people nor place, but a subject—a subject common to many ancient peoples, namely the communication of thought through distance and time by writing. Its author is Dr David Diringer, Lecturer in Semitic Epigraphy in the University of Cambridge, and Professor in the University of Florence, and founder of the Alphabet Museum, Cambridge. It is a pleasure to welcome this book for itself, and also as the first in the *Ancient Peoples and Places* series dealing with a specific aspect of antiquity.

GLYN DANIEL

ACKNOWLEDGEMENT

My profoundest thanks are due to Mr Henry Ebel,
formerly of Clare College, Cambridge, for his col-
laboration and assistance in the writing of this book.

D.D.

Introduction

LITERALLY AND CLOSELY defined, writing is the graphic counterpart of speech, the 'fixing' of spoken language in a permanent or semi-permanent form, or, in the words of a French scholar, *'une représentation visuelle et durable du langage, qui le rend transportable et conservable.'* By means of it, language is made capable of transcending the ordinary conditions of time and space. By means of it, a Babylonian merchant, ensuring himself against legal difficulties, could record the precise details of a transaction on a tablet of wet clay, subsequently baked (unaware, of course, that it would survive to find a place in the British Museum); a complete copy of Quintilian could survive, buried in rubbish and dust at the monastery of St Gall, to be found by Poggio Bracciolini; and, to take another example very much at random, Matthew Arnold was able to record the precise series of thoughts and feelings known as *Culture and Anarchy*.

Writing, as even these scattered examples indicate, is at one time the most universal and the most elusive of things. It has escaped formal study in most universities, yet every scholarly discipline touches upon it at some point, and often in matters of considerable importance. Like sunlight and the air we breathe, it is so 'common,' so 'ordinary' and so 'understood' a thing that often it is not understood at all; and the study of its history and development has suffered as a result.

Without writing, culture, which has been defined as 'a communicable intelligence,' would not exist (except, perhaps, in a form so rudimentary as to be virtually unrecognisable). Law, religion, trade, poetry, philosophy, history – all those human activities which depend upon a degree of permanence and transmission – would be, not impossible, but incalculably restricted. The possibilities inherent in oral transmission are far wider than was conceived a century or two ago, but, in comparison with the worlds opened up by the use of writing, they are bounded by fixed and absolute limits.

Nor is this importance simply a matter of scholarly hindsight. Writing was held in such esteem and awe by most ancient peoples that its invention was frequently attributed to divinities or folk-heroes. The ancient Egyptians assigned it alternatively to Thoth and Isis; the Babylonians to Nebo, son of Marduk, who was also the god of man's destiny; the Greeks to Hermes and other of the Olympians. An ancient Jewish tradition considered Moses the inventor of the Hebrew script. And many other peoples, including the Chinese, the Indians, and the pre-Columbian inhabitants of Mexico and Central America, also believed in its divine origin.

We can with justice, therefore, speak of writing as so uniquely useful and powerful a craft that to call it an 'instrument' is implicitly to understate. At a time when the distinction between subjective and objective was less clear-cut than it is today, it seemed to most men a magic power: a connotation which continued to cling to it even in the West until comparatively recent times.

WRITING
versus
LANGUAGE

As our initial definition indicates, writing presupposes the existence of spoken language. Indeed, mankind lived for an enormous period without writing of any kind, and there is no doubt that articulate speech was in use during this time. What degree of complexity it attained cannot be proven, but it must have been sufficient to cover the considerable range of activity which characterises even a pre-urban society, nomadic or settled. For thousands of years languages developed, changed and disappeared, following into extinction the peoples who spoke them, leaving behind no scrap or fragment for scholars to puzzle over or laymen to romanticise. No comparable disappearance can be cited: flint, pottery and bone can be buried, scattered or broken, and yet survive; anthropologists and archaeologists can reconstruct prehistoric villages, and even, to some extent, the habits of the men who lived in them; but the languages of those men are irrecoverably lost, and with the languages their religions, their thoughts, their myths. The evidence of burials and figurines must always remain, to a good extent, conjectural.

At some point in the comparatively recent past, within those few thousand years which have seen the real intellectual development of mankind, writing, in the sense that we understand the word today, had its origins. An analysis of first causes here is an extraordinarily difficult and touchy affair, much like analysing the 'causes' of a war or revolution: in each case those present when the phenomenon has its birth have usually little or no concern with posterity, and posterity must, in consequence, tread warily. What can be said with certainty is that there is no evidence to prove that any *complete system* of writing was employed before the middle of the fourth millennium B.C. Representational cave-paintings and carvings on small objects have been found from as early a period as the Upper Palaeolithic (some 20,000 years or more B.C.), as well as circles and other symbols, full of variety and distinction. Some of these were apparently used as property marks, or for similar purposes. But they are not in any way complete (that is, established and systematic) forms of writing, nor can any connection be traced between them and the ancient systems we know. The ultimate roots of the latter are in every case matters of conjecture.

We can perhaps say that all forms of graphic inscription, however crude or refined, have their roots in the central and universal human need to *communicate* and *express*. Nevertheless, a clear distinction must be made, if our subject is to be rendered at all practicable, between what we shall henceforth call *embryo-writing* and *writing proper*. The prehistoric painting and sculpture which we find from the Upper Palaeolithic onwards was partly an attempt at expression and communication, and partly, as we shall see, a kind of sympathetic magic (it is im⁄possible to separate completely the two functions). Such forms have continued to spring up well into historic times, and long after the appearance even of alphabetic writing. But most of these devices, ancient and modern, are isolated, arbitrary and unsystematic in the way that they 'fix' language and ideas, and have little to do with the systematic and (in the fullest sense of the word) *conscious* writing which we find for the first time in the fourth millennium B.C.

This is not to say that everything before that time must be neglected: on the contrary, anything which throws light upon man's earliest attempts at expression and communication, how⁄ever distant it may be from the study of actual scripts, cannot but assist our understanding of writing and its development, and cannot but be worthy of examination. Even the evidence of modern anthropology should not be neglected when, in examining recent or contemporary 'primitive' communities and peoples, it gives us new insights into the workings of many rudimentary forms of communication. But a line must be drawn, and we should not, in reacting against oversimplified ideas about 'primitive' and 'rude' stages of civilisation, go to the opposite extreme, and lump together in the category of 'writing' every form of graphic expression used by man.

Writing, as we understand it, is a conscious activity, in⁄tricately and inseparably bound up with the development, comparatively recent, of man's conscious intellect. The esta⁄blishment or stabilisation of a written script – cuneiform, or Chinese, or Hittite hieroglyphic – implies a degree of con⁄sciousness towards language so much larger than that of, say, Palaeolithic man, as to amount to a difference in kind.

DEVELOP⁄
MENT
AND SPREAD
OF SCRIPTS

At the risk of seeming paradoxical, a word must now be said about the 'progressive' fallacy, of which so much has been written in other contexts. It is a fallacy inherent not only in modern liberal habits of thought, but, alas, in the very struc⁄

ture of our language, and most of all in the language and metho⸝
dology of modern scholarship. Some would banish the word
progress itself to the hinterlands: but *development* and *evolution*
remain behind to plague them, with their tinge of something
very similar. Difficulties such as these – above all, the assump⸝
tion that all change is necessarily 'progressive' – are especially
inherent in our present subject. A very helpful pictographic
diagram, carelessly used or interpreted, can give the impression
of a vast river of script churning purposefully and irrevocably to⸝
wards the modern alphabet. Such misunderstandings must be
anticipated now if we are to be free to use a good many common
verbs in later chapters, and to introduce any concept of progress.

The struggle for survival is the principal condition for the
existence of a script, as for so many other things; and *on the
whole*, barring severe interference of any kind, a script will
'evolve' in the direction of simplicity and utility (which, in the
case of writing not intended for mere physical impressiveness,
is *ipso facto* an improvement), and the fittest scripts will survive:
the scripts which are most useful and adaptable, and which
best meet the needs of the men who use them. Yet, in the course
of history, how much 'severe interference' there has been! The
invasion of a land by foreign people may have untold con⸝
sequences in obliterating a native script, introducing a new one,
or in making the invaders literate for the first time. Sometimes
the use of a particular script for ritual and religious purposes –
as, say, in the Rabbinic, Samaritan and Coptic transmission
of Biblical texts – effectually removes it from ordinary forms of
competition and use, ensuring that it will survive at least as
long as those who revere it. The movement of religious con⸝
version has often introduced a script into use throughout vast
land⸝areas, to which it may perhaps have penetrated without
such 'severe interference,' but only at an immensely slower pace:
and good examples of this are the transmissions of the Arabic
alphabet to all the lands from Spain to Indonesia.

Moreover, there have been cases in which, without any external interference being visible, a script did not move towards
greater utility and simplicity but developed in a quite contrary
direction. Thus, Chinese writing, which has been in a kind
of linguistic straitjacket since its time of origin, has today some
tens of thousands of symbols, of which 3,000 to 5,000 are actually employed by Chinese scholars. The Egyptian hieroglyphic
script, in the course of its several thousand years of existence,
became progressively more cluttered with auxiliary signs
which, though their intent had at one time been to ensure a
correct reading of various words, were now inserted quite use-
lessly and redundantly (though they were undoubtedly very
decorative!). And other, similar examples could be cited. So
that there are many factors, aside from the ideal usefulness of a
script, which determine its development, spread and survival.

In addition to all this, we must keep in mind that the most
rudimentary forms of communication are not always earlier
in time than systematic scripts: a fact which the methodology
of our subject often obscures. Indeed, such rudimentary forms
have continued to spring up – and, in their own ways, to
develop – long after the appearance of alphabetic writing, and
some remain in use to this day. From here it is only a short
step to saying that various kinds of writing often develop con-
temporaneously in different or even in the same parts of the
world, and that at any point in history a cross-section of the
writings in use would reveal a very vast panorama, with little
in it of the false clarity of retrospect. From an imaginary vantage
point in the stratosphere we would, without any previous
knowledge, be hard put to tell which script was doomed to
rapid oblivion, which to a steady and prolonged but not very
spectacular existence, and which to a sudden acceleration of
fortune. Above all, we would see little of the 'inevitability'
which a survey of the sort undertaken in this book may seem
to suggest.

All this is preliminary and cautionary. It is in no way a throwing-up of the hands, or a denial that we can ever point to a straightforward example of progress in the history of writing. Such examples there have in fact been. As we have already implied, the appearance of systematic scripts, of which cuneiform was (so far as we know) the first, represented an immense stride forward in the history of mankind, more profound in its own way than the discovery of fire or the wheel: for while the latter have facilitated man's control over his physical environment, writing has been the foundation for the development of his consciousness and his intellect, his comprehension of himself and the world about him, and, in the very widest sense possible, of his critical spirit – indeed, of all that we today regard as his unique heritage and his *raison d'être*. Only the most recalcitrant and quixotic of intuitionists could find in all this a Bad Thing.

A second, more specific, and perhaps more dramatic example of progress is the development of alphabetic writing. The Alphabet, as we shall see in more detail in Chapter V, almost certainly had its origin at a single point in history, and in a specific, if hitherto uncertain, place in the Near East, probably in Palestine or Syria. It was, historically, the last major form of writing to appear, and it is the most highly developed, the most convenient, and the most easily adaptable system of writing ever invented. From its point and time of origin it moved on to become the basis for all Semitic, Indian, Greek, Latin, Slavonic and modern Western scripts, as well as of several others we shall have occasion to mention later. It moved on, that is, towards what has been called the 'triumph' or 'conquest' of the Alphabet: phrases somewhat too military for so great a benefaction to mankind. Here, too, keeping in mind the qualifications and reservations just made, the concept of progress is integral to our subject.

And lastly, many examples could be cited of scripts which

ALPHABETIC
WRITING

have moved in the direction of greater usefulness and utility during their 'lifetimes': most often in a slow, sometimes millen_{nia}long evolution at the hands of countless generations of scribes; sometimes in a single conscious leap, as in the establishment of Persian cuneiform or the Turkish (Latin) alphabet.

WRITING
AS A FIELD
OF STUDY

We may, for the moment, broaden out the definition with which we began this introduction, and take writing to mean the conveyance of ideas or sounds by marks on some suitable medium ranging from stone to wood, clay, metal, leather, linen, parchment, paper and wax (a definition which would include embryowriting as well). Although, as we have mentioned, the history of writing as such is not studied in most universities, it does form the principal basis for two other important branches of research: and since the real prevalence of extant documents written on such surfaces as paper and parchment is chronologically later in time than the prevalence of inscriptions in harder materials, the division between these two falls quite naturally into what we know as *epigraphy* and *palaeography*.

Epigraphy, ordinarily subdivided into such specialities as Greek epigraphy, Latin epigraphy and Hebrew epigraphy, is the study which deals principally with ancient inscriptions cut, engraved or moulded on such materials as stone, metal and clay. Such study includes the problems of decipherment and interpretation. Palaeography, which is subdivided in a parallel fashion into specialities like Greek, Latin and Hebrew palaeography, deals principally with writing which is painted or traced on to soft materials such as paper, parchment, papyrus, linen and wax, using such tools as a stylus, brush, reed or pen. Once again, decipherment and interpretation of texts are an integral part of the discipline.

The study of palaeography has been and is of the greatest practical importance for textual criticism of all kinds, for classical philology, for ancient and medieval history, and for other branches of historical science. The study of epigraphy, on the other hand, has revolutionised our knowledge of the ancient world, and has led to the rediscovery and reconstruction of entire civilisations.

The fragmented study of writing is grounded at least partly, therefore, in these differences between materials. Certain branches of the study, however, form parts of other departments of learning. Hieroglyphic, hieratic and demotic writing (the three ancient Egyptian scripts) are ordinarily comprehended in the general discipline of Egyptology, cuneiform in Assyriology, 'primitive' writing in anthropology and ethnology, and so forth. Philology and glottology – studies of language – may also deal with writing, when and if the latter is relevant to the issue at hand (as it very frequently is). Graphology, 'the science of writing', is more concerned with the subject from the biological and psychological points of view than in terms of its history.

Used by and sometimes cutting across these various fields are a number of classifications which attempt to group different writings according to their nature, and according to the stage of development which each has attained. Some of these classifications are very useful, but all must be taken with caution: they are matters of convenience, not hardandfast lines of demarcation. The categories (all of which have to do with true writing, not embryowriting) are:

Pictography or *picturewriting*. This is the most rudimentary stage of true writing. It is the first important step beyond embryowriting in that it is no longer restricted to the recording of single, disconnected images, but is capable of representing the sequential stages or ideas of a simple narrative. The action is recorded by a series of more or less straightforwardly representational pictures or sketches, each one of which is called a *pictogram*. Picturewritings can be expressed orally in any language without alteration of content, since the pictures do not stand for specific sounds. Intrinsic phonetism (from Greek *phonê*, 'voice') is still absent: though each of the objects or things re

CLASSIFI
CATION OF
SCRIPTS

presented did of course have an oral name of some kind among those who did the drawings. Pictography of various kinds was used by many prehistoric peoples, including those of Egypt, Mesopotamia, Phoenicia, Crete, Spain, southern France, China, America, and Africa. They have continued to be used in modern times by inhabitants of Central Africa, South-east Asia, Siberia and elsewhere.

Ideographic writing. In appearance a highly-developed kind of picture-writing, ideographic writing is really very much more: it is in fact the first step in rendering a script capable of conveying abstractions, subtleties and multiple associations. The pictograms now, as before, can represent simply the things they show, but may connote as well the underlying ideas or conceptions with which those things are bound up. Thus, whereas in simple pictography a circle might represent the sun, in ideographic writing it might also stand for heat, light, a god associated with the sun, or the word 'day'. In addition, an animal might be ideographically depicted, not by a complete representation, but by a sketch of the head alone: a part calls up the complex whole. The individual symbols are called *ideograms*, and they show a striking similarity in many rudimentary scripts otherwise separated in time and space. 'Pure' ideographic writing has been found among the indigenous inhabitants of North America, Central America, Africa, Polynesia and Australia, as well as among the Yukaghirs of north-eastern Siberia. In dealing with ideographic writing, we still do not generally have to do with *complete systems* of writing.

Analytic transitional scripts. The writings of the ancient Mesopotamians, Egyptians, Cretans and Hittites have frequently and incorrectly been called 'ideographic'. In fact, though they may very well have been ideographic in their origins, the very earliest examples known to us of each of these scripts are already only partly ideographic, having a phonetic element as well: the two forms being combined in various ways. For lack of a better term, these forms of writing have been labelled 'transi-tional,' in that they stand somewhere between pure ideographic and pure phonetic writing. It should be remembered, however, that some of these systems of writing lasted for three thousand years or more, and that they can be regarded as 'transitional' only within the broadest of historical perspectives. The word 'analytic' simply indicates a script whose basic units (however these are represented) are *words*.

Phonetic scripts. In 'pure' ideographic writing, there is still no connection between the depicted symbol and the spoken name for it: the symbols can be read with equal facility in any language. In phonetic writing we have, for the first time, the graphic counterpart of speech. Each element in such a system of writing corresponds to a sound or sounds in the language which is being represented. A direct and inseparable relation-ship has therefore been set up between written and spoken language: the former can only be explained or read through a knowledge of the latter. The single signs used in phonetic writing may be of any shape, and there need be no connection between the external form of the symbol and the sound it represents.

This brings us to the last great division of our subject: for phonetic writing (if it is in a 'pure' form, and not simply an element in a transitional script) may be either syllabic or alpha-betic. Syllabic forms of writing (or *syllabaries*) are ultimately based upon the fact that the smallest unit into which any spo-ken word or series of sounds can be subdivided is the syllable. The idea of using single symbols to represent syllables seems to have arisen at various times in many parts of the world, though few scripts ever managed to shed completely the ideograms of an earlier stage and so to become 'pure' syllabaries. A flexible method of writing, far less cumbersome and far more exact than ideograms, a syllabary can nevertheless be an unwieldy system when in a particular language syllables contain more than one or two consonants. Thus, although it would be a simple matter to represent syllabically a word like *fa⁄mi⁄ly*, the word 'strength' would have to be written *se⁄te⁄re⁄ne⁄ge⁄the*, and, since each syllable would be represented by some single differentiated sign, the total number of symbols in the script would still be comparatively large.

Alphabetic writing. Though technically a subdivision of pho⁄netic writing, alphabetic writing has within the past three thousand years assumed such importance as to deserve a cate⁄gory of its own. The enormous advantages implicit in using letters to represent single sounds (rather than ideas or even sylla⁄bles) are obvious, and need no prolonged restatement here. With its 22 or 24 or 26 signs, the Alphabet is the most flexible and useful method of writing ever invented, and, from its origins in the Near East, has become the nearly universal basis for the scripts employed by civilised peoples, passing from language to language with a minimum of difficulty. No other system of writing has had so extensive, so intricate and so interesting a history.

The division and presentation of the history of writing in this book is partly historical (that is, chronological), partly na⁄tional (or ethnic), and partly by *genre* or type. One division suggests itself immediately: that between non⁄alphabetic and alphabetic scripts, with the latter following historically and logically upon the former. This, with the addition of a pre⁄liminary chapter on embryo⁄writings and other early forms of communication, and separate chapters on the scripts of China, and of ancient Mexico and Central America, has been the method adopted. In the three chapters on non⁄alphabetic writ⁄ing, some allowance must be made for distortion. Here the division has first been made by area (the ancient Near East, the Far East, and pre⁄Columbian America), within which sub⁄divisions scripts have been treated approximately in their order of origin, insofar as this order is known today. Thus, cuneiform is treated in its entirety, from its beginnings through its death as a script, before the earliest Egyptian writing is dealt with. Since cuneiform lingered on into the Christian era, and the last known example of Egyptian demotic writing is dated A.D. 476, there is in this case as in others a good deal of complex overlapping. The reader should occasionally make a quiet mental correction for it.

Such subjects as numerical and musical notation, shorthand, calligraphy and printing are of course relevant to the history of writing and worthy of treatment in their own right. The exigencies of a book of this size have made it impossible, however, to deal with them in a systematic fashion.

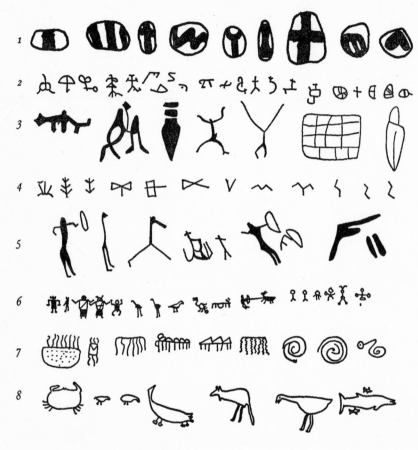

Fig. 1 *Prehistoric conventionalised figures and geometric symbols: 1, painted pebbles of the mesolithic Azilian culture, painted with peroxide or iron, from Mas d'Azil, Ariège, South France; 2, geometric signs from Spain; 3, conventionalised figures and signs from Italy; 4, symbols on masonry and pottery from Crete; 5, conventionalised figures from North African rock paintings; 6–7, petroglyphs from California; 8, petroglyphs from Australia*

CHAPTER I

Primitive means of communication: Embryo-writing

IN DEALING WITH the very first precursors of writing we cut across several categories. The earliest embryo-writings, scratched, drawn or painted by men of the Upper Palaeolithic on the walls of caves, could be treated under the history of art, the history of magic, or the history of writing. This is only to say, of course, that they belong to a yet undivided form of human activity from which later, more specialised forms have gradually separated themselves; and that we can at best approximate, by long-drawn and self-defeating explanations, the kind of *Weltanschauung* which produced them.

The earliest embryo-writings – schematic figures of animals, geometric patterns, crude pictures of objects of various kinds – have been found in north-eastern Spain, south-western France, the eastern Mediterranean, northern Europe and North Africa. Some of these go back to about 20,000 B.C. They were not intended for expression, communication or 'decoration' in the modern sense, but were probably bound up with sympathetic magic and ritual practices of some sort. Thus, the striking and famous cave-paintings of bison and other animals found in and near the Pyrenees may have been intended as a ritual gesture to ensure good hunting. Yet even this is almost certainly an oversimplification, as any modern discussion of magic is liable to be.

It is interesting to note the degree of conventionalisation and geometricism which is already present in even those rock-paintings (*petrograms*) and rock-engravings (*petroglyphs*) which are intended to represent recognisable things: a man may be captured quite dynamically in three rapid strokes, a bird reduced to a triangle, two curved lines and a dozen straight ones:

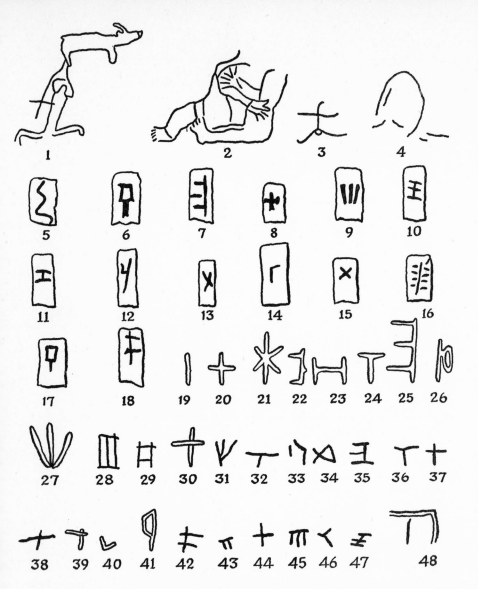

Fig. 2 *Petroglyphs and geometric symbols on rocks, masonry and pottery from Palestine: 1–4, rock engravings from Transjordan; 5–26, geometric signs engraved on building-stones, from the ancient Hebrew royal palaces at Megiddo (5–18) and Samaria (19–26); 27–48, geometric signs engraved on ancient pottery, from Tell Jemmeh (27–30) and Tell el-Ḥesy (31–48)*

so that it is probably fruitless to pursue at any length the question as to whether or not straightforwardly geometrical embryo-writing 'developed out of' representational drawing. Putting the question in this way poses a quite false dichotomy. The element of geometricism is present from the very beginning, and seems as natural a form of expression as a more 'realistic' technique.

Fig. 3 New Zealand petroglyphs   Scale: feet

Despite their incredibly wide geographical range, and the fact that they span many millennia of recorded and unrecorded history (those in the rock shelters of North Kimberley, Australia, still serve a religious function for the natives), all embryo-writings have this in common: that the impressions or ideas they convey are invariably *static*. This is not to impute to them any lack of what we must call 'artistic merit': some of them are indeed very brilliant creations, and those of the Pyrenees especially have received a great deal of attention from modern art

Plates 1, 2

29

historians and critics. By *static* we mean only that, being dis-connected and arbitrary images, they cannot convey to us even the simplest ideas, or the simplest sequence of narrative. They can convey to us the power, dynamism and movement im-plicit in the form of a bison or a mammoth, and do this bril-liantly: but they cannot form these single, static impressions into a discourse. We could perhaps say that in embryo-writings the nouns are present, but that verbs, adverbs and prepositions are lacking.

Fig. 1

Purposes of sympathetic magic or ritual probably also ac-count for the painted river-pebbles of the so-called Azilian Culture (from Mas d'Azil, Ariège, in southern France), and for the petrograms and petroglyphs – geometric signs and con-ventionalised human figures or representation of animals – which have been found in Neolithic and later tombs through-

Fig. 2, 3

out the Mediterranean area, and indeed the world over.

With the transition to pictography – a transition by no means necessary or inevitable – we come to deal for the first time with a form of true writing, though still not with esta-blished systems of any kind. Picture-writings from prehistoric times have been found throughout the world – in Europe, South Africa, the Soviet Union, Australia, India, Polynesia, Melanesia, Micronesia, Crete, Egypt, Palestine, Syria, the Ba-hamas, North and South America – and new discoveries are reported each year. From pictography of some sort there de-veloped the greatest of the ancient scripts, whose history we shall begin to examine in the next chapter.

MEMORY AID DEVICES

This brief survey of the earliest precursors of writing would not be complete without some mention of other rudimentary forms for recording, expressing and communicating ideas. Many of these have existed alongside embryo- and picturewritings, and some have continued to be used in cultures which had already developed quite advanced scripts. Although these methods of communication cannot really be classified under the history of writing, they help to give us some idea of the milieu or milieus out of which many scripts sprang, and of the way in which, early in the history of mankind, what we know today to have been the precursors of writing represented only one among many alternative methods of communication.

One of the commonest devices for recalling to mind a task or errand is to tie a knot in a handkerchief, a mnemonic device which has been employed by a variety of peoples and cultures. The simplest application of knots as an aid to memory has usually been in keeping a record of numbers, an interesting example of which is related by Herodotus (iv, 98, trans. Sélincourt):

> Soon after, [Darius] called a meeting of the Ionian commanders and showed them a long leather strap in which he had tied sixty knots. Men of Ionia, he said... I want you to take this strap, and every day undo one of the knots, beginning with the day on which you see me start my march against the Scythians. Should I fail to return before all the knots have given out, you are at liberty to sail home...

The Catholic rosary is a similar mnemonic device, though one which has acquired religious overtones above and beyond its purely functional purpose.

The knot-device forms the basis for the Peruvian *quipus* (or *quipos*) which were found in such general use by the Spanish *conquistadores*. They consisted of a number of threads or cords of different lengths, thicknesses and colours, generally of twisted wool, suspended from a top-band or cross-bar. Though ordinarily employed for keeping numerical records of various kinds, they could also be used to convey news of recent events or official edicts. (The Peruvian Incas, as far as we know, used no writing.)

Fig. 4

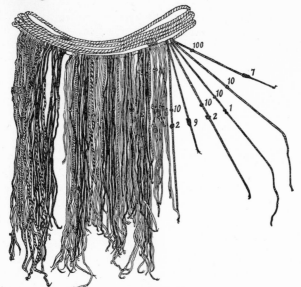

Fig. 4   Peruvian quipus *from the Inca city of Pachamac*

Similar to these devices are the *aroko* epistles of the modern Jebu and other Nigerian tribes, which consist of cowrie shells strung together in different combinations and directions; while related mnemonic methods, including knotted cords, were used until modern times by the Li of Hainan and the Sonthals of Bengal, by some indigenous inhabitants of Polynesia, southern Peru, central and western Africa, and California, and by inhabitants of the Riukiu, Solomon, Caroline, Pelew and Marquesan Islands.

Another method which has been widely used at various times as an aid in conveying messages is the notched stick. Like the *quipus* and almost all other devices of this kind, these sticks are today unintelligible except where still in use by contemporary 'primitive' tribes. All such methods of communication are in effect codes, the keys to the decipherment of which are carried in the heads of those who use them. The 'key' to the ancient Peruvian *quipus* was clearly very elaborate and systematic, since these were used not only as simple numerical records but for the transmission of more complex forms of information. Notched sticks, on the other hand, are often incised in the presence of a messenger to whom the significance of each notch is verbally emphasised: so that sticks of this kind may be of the very simplest kind of mnemonic device, and in no way real records.

Notched sticks of various sorts have been employed not only by some 'primitive' peoples of Australia, North America, western Africa, China, Mongolia, and South-east Asia, but also in ancient Scandinavia, England (the so-called 'tally-sticks'), Italy and Russia. The Khas of Indo-China still keep their accounts and transmit messages by means of small pieces of bamboo, marked with notches at closer or longer intervals.

An interesting example of a similar form of memory-aid, still used in England during the lifetime of Dryden, is described by Alfred Moorhouse: the 'clog almanacs' of the English Midlands, found especially in the neighbourhood of Staffordshire:

> These were four-sided blocks of wood with notches cut on the edges to represent the days of the year. Primarily they were almanacs of the ecclesiastical year. Festivals and saints' days were distinguished by signs – for example, St David's Day by the figure of a harp.

There are forms of communication similar to those already mentioned, which have in addition a strong symbolic element. An example is the *wampum* of the North American Iroquois: Fig. 5

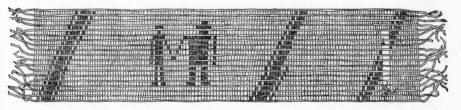

Fig. 5 Wampum *belt. The* famous Penn *wampum, which symbolises the treaty between William Penn (the founder of Pennsylvania) and the North-American Iroquois*

a broad belt consisting of shells or beads strung together to form a picture of some sort, usually representing an occurrence of considerable moment. It was worn as an ornament or girdle, and was sometimes also used as money. (The word '*Wampum*' is still occasionally used, in the United States, as a colloquial synonym for 'money'.)

Some methods of communication are almost completely symbolic, and are invariably far less wieldy than any of those we have already mentioned. Thus, the Lu-tze, on the Tibeto-Chinese frontier, might at one time have dispatched a message in the form of a piece of chicken liver, three pieces of chicken fat and a chili – all wrapped together in red paper. The import of this would be, 'prepare to fight at once.' The Bangala people of the Upper Congo still send personal tokens of various kinds – knives, pipes, spears – to emphasise the importance of a verbal message: the tokens are subsequently returned by the messenger.

Mention should be made, finally, of a very ancient *genre* which it is impossible to classify under any other category or heading. This includes such devices as brands, heraldic emblems, trade-marks, seals and property-marks. The use of such emblems has been and still is so universal that a complete list is impossible, and a partial one would seem a bit absurd. Many of the symbols found in embryo-writings were probably used in this way; while definite markings of this kind have been found on ancient pottery and masonry in Palestine, Crete, Egypt, Cyprus, Transylvania, and elsewhere.

cf. Figs 1, 2

Analytic scripts of the ancient Near East

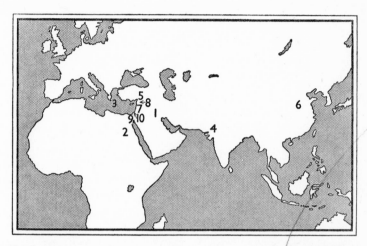

Fig. 6 Main systems of writing c. 3000–1000 B.C. 1, Cuneiform scripts (Mesopo-tamia and surrounding countries); 2, Egyptian scripts—hieroglyphic, hieratic, demotic; 3, Cretan scripts; 4, Indus Valley script; 5, Hittite hieroglyphic script (Asia Minor and Northern Syria); 6, Chinese scripts; 7, Byblos pseudo-hieroglyphic script; 8, Ugarit (Râs Shamrah) cuneiform alphabet; 9, Palaeo-Sinaitic script; 10, North Semitic alphabet

CUNEIFORM WRITING

CUNEIFORM (from Latin *cuneus,* 'wedge,' and *forma,* 'shape') is the most ancient system of writing we know of today. Since its decipherment in the nineteenth century it has been subjected to an immense amount of study and specula-tion; but its origins remain obscure.

Some time around the middle of the fourth millennium B.C. a people of unknown ethnic and linguistic affiliation whom we know as the Sumerians entered the southern part of Mesopota-

Fig. 6

mia and conquered the area from its original inhabitants. From the last centuries of the fourth millennium, they were for 1500 years the dominant cultural group of the Near East, producing a highly developed literature and leaving behind records and documents of a large and complex system of law, administration, trade and religion.

ORIGIN AND
DEVELOP-
MENT OF
CUNEIFORM
WRITING

At some time in the first five hundred years of their occupation, the Sumerians began to use the writing which eventually developed into cuneiform. It is uncertain whether they actually invented it; its ultimate source may have been earlier Semitic inhabitants of the land, or it may have been brought into Mesopotamia from some other place. The problem of its origin is complicated by the fact that the early Sumerian script bears resemblances of undetermined significance to the early linear script of the Elamites, to Egyptian hieroglyphic writing, and to the Indus Valley script.

Whatever the exact nature of its origins, our knowledge of the earliest Sumerian writing is based upon a singularly rich find made at Uruk (the Biblical Erech, north-west of Ur) early in the second quarter of this century: over one thousand tablets and fragments inscribed in a crude pictographic script which, in all probability, represents the Sumerian language.

Plates 3, 4

In its earliest form, then, cuneiform writing was not *cuneiform* (that is, 'wedge-shaped') at all but a kind of picture-writing, with the cumbersomeness which pictography always implies; approximately nine hundred different symbols were found in the stratum of Uruk known as ivb, and even this total may be only a fraction of those actually in use at the time.

The earliest inscriptions found at Uruk are pictographic in the very simplest way, containing no ideograms at all. But at a second stage we find that the transition to an ideographic *and* phonetic script had already begun: the solar disc now representing the concepts of 'day' and 'time,' and the sun itself. The phonetisation of the Sumerian script had begun at the same time: in the second oldest 'lode' of Sumerian writing, the Uruk III stratum, tablets were found on which the *arrow* sign stands for both the Sumerian word *ti*, 'arrow,' and *ti*, 'life' – the identity of pronunciation being the only connecting link.

Thus, it is incorrect to speak of the Sumerian script as being at any point (so far as we know) purely ideographic. It was first a form of picture-writing; and then, without a break, became what we have defined as a transitional script. The ultimate decipherment of the earlier pictographic writings found at Uruk may in fact indicate that phonetisation began at an even earlier stage.

At the same time that these changes were taking place, the script was changing in its external form as well. The pictures began to be simplified and conventionalised, retaining just enough of their original features to be recognisable. The script became linear: began to be written, that is, in simply drawn lines. And (what was to be the most important factor in the development of cuneiform) clay, so easily obtainable in Mesopotamia, became increasingly the material on which writing was done. To this development, too, we owe the preservation of so many Sumerian records, since even when left unbaked, to harden in the sun (as was the case with many of the tablets), clay is one of the most durable of materials. Other, more perishable surfaces may have been used at the same time – wood, or some form of papyrus – but this cannot be ascertained.

Around 3200 B.C., some Sumerian scribes found it convenient, for purposes of writing, to turn the clay tablets in such a way that the finished symbols seem to be lying on their backs: though in such inscriptions as were scratched into stone or metal the older positions were retained for several centuries more. Eventually, however, even these were inscribed at an angle of ninety degrees. These rotated symbols were those which were eventually conventionalised into the characters we may properly call cuneiform.

Fig. 7

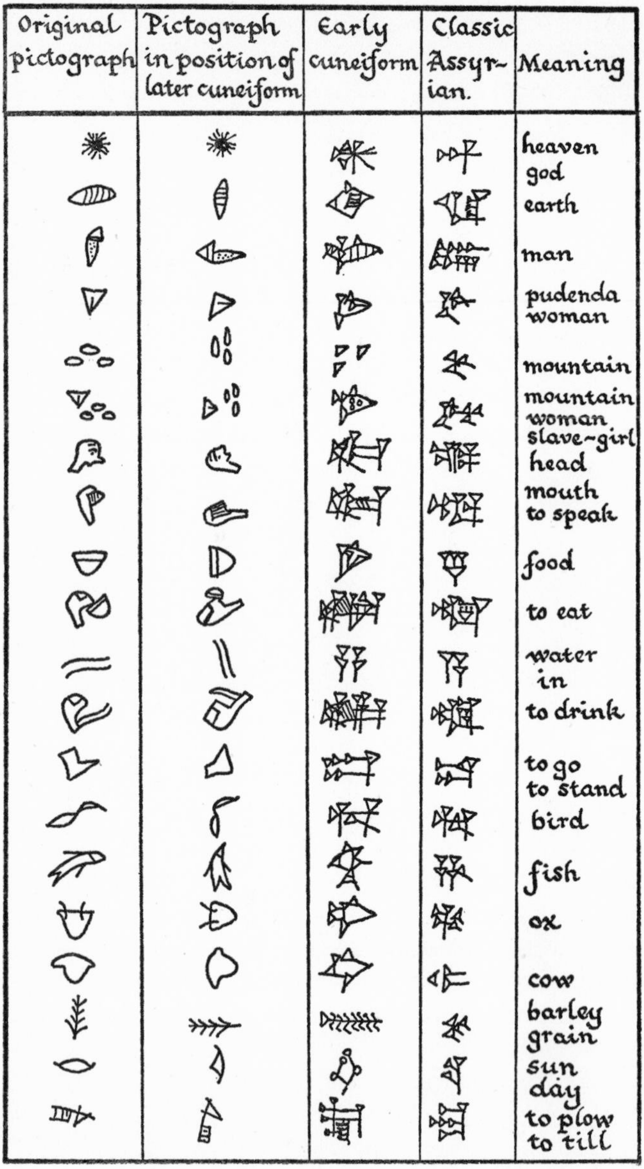

Original pictograph	Pictograph in position of later cuneiform	Early cuneiform	Classic Assyrian.	Meaning
				heaven god
				earth
				man
				pudenda woman
				mountain
				mountain woman slave-girl head
				mouth to speak
				food
				to eat
				water in
				to drink
				to go to stand
				bird
				fish
				ox
				cow
				barley grain
				sun day
				to plow to till

Fig. 7 Development of cuneiform symbols from pictographs to Classic Assyrian

The crucial point in this development was the change from the script we have mentioned to the characteristic wedge-shaped strokes used for all Sumerian, Assyrian and Babylonian cuneiform writing. Working in wet clay, the Sumerian scribes found that characters could be drawn much more neatly and efficiently by *impressing* them into the surface than by scratching. Anyone who has ever tried to inscribe a design into a clay pot or figurine before firing will appreciate the point. In any case, the newer method proved excellent for short, straight, relatively thick lines, at the same time that it was most unsatisfactory for the drawing of curves, circles, and lines of any length or fineness. As a result, all the latter were eventually replaced by short, straight strokes in a vertical, horizontal or oblique position.

These strokes were made with the edge of a broad-headed *stylus*: a straight length of reed, bone, hard wood or metal. The scribe, as represented on Assyrian monuments, held the stylus in his closed fist and pressed it into the wet clay. The direction of writing was from left to right, the scribe holding the stylus in his right hand to avoid smudging what he had written: and the natural inequality of pressure which this process entailed produced the characteristic wedge-shape of the stroke.

The wedge shape of these characters, called 'triangles' by those who used them, gradually became more marked, and were finally standardised into the script which we know today as cuneiform: by which time very little indeed remained of the original pictograms from which it had sprung. Once they had been standardised, cuneiform characters, though they owed their peculiar shape completely to the mechanics of working in wet clay, were cut by the Sumerians on stone, metal, glass and other hard materials. Cuneiform was to reach its physical perfection as a script at the hands of the Assyrian royal scribes, whose calligraphy is beautiful even to modern eyes.

We must now go back a step, and resume our narration of the development of cuneiform as a representation of the Sumerian language. With the continued influx of phoneticism, the range of expression of the cuneiform symbols became very wide: indeed, the script soon included signs for four out of the five Sumerian vowels, a fact which did much to make Sumerian cuneiform a flexible form of communication. With its partially ideographic, partially phonetic origins, however, the script retained a number of confusing ambiguities. Some of the symbols were *polyphones*, having more than one phonetic value; others were *homophones*, having similar phonetic values, but representing entirely different meanings. Thus, to give an example of a polyphone, the triple wedge-stroke which was ultimately derived from the pictogram for *mountain* acquired a total of ten possible phonetic values – *gin, kur, kin, lat, mat, mad, nat, nad, shat, shad* – and four ideographic values as well. The homophone *gar*, on the other hand, could be represented by fourteen different symbols, each of which meant a completely different thing; *si* by fourteen; and *tu* by a total of sixteen.

In order to remove these ambiguities, a class of signs which we call *determinatives* were introduced by the Sumerian scribes. These were placed before or after words whose meaning might be ambiguous, were not themselves pronounced, and served to indicate the general class or category to which the word belonged – e.g. birds, numbers, male proper nouns, deities, countries, plural form, and so forth. These determinatives were not newly invented, but were drawn from the general stock of ideograms already in the script. Unwieldy as this system may seem to us, it served quite well for the Sumerians: and we, who have nothing more than what the anthropologist Malinowski called 'the context of situation' to assist us in deciphering the three or more possible meanings of 'low', 'hand' and 'left', may be objects of equal wonder in half a millennium.

A second form of determinative was the phonetic complement, a sign used as a phonogram which, when added to a polyphone, made clear the particular phonetic value which was needed by repeating its pronounced ending. This may best be explained, perhaps, by a very hypothetical example. Let us imagine that our pronounced word 'sugar' were written as a symbol *&£&*, but that *&£&*, being a polyphone, could equally well stand for the pronounced words 'pot', 'horse', 'threshing' and 'pitfall'. A second symbol, *@!@*, stands for the syllable *ar*. Hence, when we wish to convey the idea of 'sugar' in written form, and wish to prevent the reader from thinking (even for a moment) that we had sold a pound of pot or a pound of horse, we combine the two symbols by writing *&£&-@!@*. Someone who had just learned our language but was not quite fluent in it would, when he came upon this symbol, go through something like the following logical process: (1) the symbol seems to read *&£&-ar;* (2) hence the word desired at this point is that word, represented by *&£&*, which ends in *ar;* (3) hence the word must be *sugar*. For anyone versed in the language, of course, this process would be nearly instantaneous.

Phonetic complements were also used by the Sumerians to clarify the meaning of an ideogram when this had become diversified – when, for instance, the symbol for 'leg' had also come to represent the related meanings 'to go' and 'to stand'.

Some time around the middle of the third millennium B.C., a thousand years after their entry into Mesopotamia, the writing of the Sumerians was taken over by the Semites who lived in the TigrisEuphrates Valley – the Akkadians, i.e. the Babylonians and Assyrians. For well over two thousand years it remained in some form their script, and flourished proportionately in periods of great vigour and expansion. Under Hammurabi, in the late eighteenth century B.C., cuneiform became the instrument of the great classical age of Babylonian literature and science: the period in which nearly all extant Babylonian literature was written down, and in which an advanced and thriving state of commerce and administration was reflected in thousands

AKKADIANS

Plates 5, 6

of letters on thousands of clay tablets, many of which have survived. The Code of Hammurabi, whose anticipation of much Mosaic legislation caused such a ripple of shock and surprise when it was first revealed to the world, is the most famous (but not the earliest) example of a legal system – a concept of law – made possible by the development of an established and versatile script.

Plate 8
During the Babylonian period, the number of symbols in cuneiform became stabilised at about six or seven hundred – six vowel sounds, ninety-seven simple ('open') syllables (*di, du, da,* etc.), over two hundred slightly more complex ('closed') syllables (*sun, dam, bar,* etc.), and approximately three hundred ideograms.

Plate 7
Between the ninth and seventh centuries B.C., the libraries of the Assyrian kings were stocked with tens of thousands of exquisitely engraved clay tablets, many of which were recovered in the excavation of Nineveh. The fields covered include religion, mythology, law, history, magic, science, mathematics, medicine and astronomy. Very fine Assyrian dictionaries were found, larger and more comprehensive than their Babylonian equivalents. Most impressive of all, perhaps, were the complete records made by the Assyrian kings of their campaigns and activities. These were impressed in the minutest possible cuneiform script on hollow cylinders or prisms with six, seven, eight or even ten faces. The complement which some of these chronicles offer to Biblical narratives ('confirmation' has already fallen into ill-repute in this context) is by now a matter of common knowledge.

SPREAD OF
CUNEIFORM
WRITING
In the second millennium B.C. (to jump back for a moment) the Akkadian language became the *lingua franca* of the ancient Near East, and cuneiform attained a corresponding importance. This has been confirmed by the cuneiform tablets found at Tell el-Amarna in Egypt, at Boghazköy in Asia Minor, and, indeed, throughout the Near East. It was during this period

and afterwards that the use of cuneiform was taken over by the Kassites, the Hittites, the Mitanni, the Hurrians, the Urartu, the Canaanites, the Persians, and, probably, by the local popu-lation of Cappadocia as well. In some cases cuneiform was adapted to the existing language with considerable alteration; in others, less modification was necessary; while some peoples took it over with the Akkadian language.

A separate word should be said about the transmission of cuneiform writing from the Sumerians to the Elamites, which took place at about the same time that the script was passed on to the Akkadians – or perhaps, as some scholars maintain, even earlier. The Biblical *Elam* (corresponding to Assyrian and Babylonian *Elamtu* or *Elamu*, and to Greek *Elymais*) was the ancient name for the country situated to the north of the Persian Gulf and to the east of the Lower Tigris. Inhabited by a people neither Semitic nor Indo-European, who spoke agglutinative dialects probably related to the Caucasian group of languages, this area produced a civilisation comparable to those of the Sumerians and Akkadians. In the latter part of the fourth millennium B.C., the Elamites possessed an indigenous script, of which nine inscriptions in stone and several hundred clay tablets have been found. The characters of this script, which has been partially deciphered, are geometric and linear, generally moving from left to right; they are almost certainly derived from earlier pictographic symbols, examples of which have not, however, been found. This early script, called proto-Elamite or Early Elamite, appears to be related in some way to early cuneiform, but the exact nature of this relationship is uncertain.

At a later period, just before or just after the middle of the third millennium B.C., the Elamites abandoned this indigenous script and adopted (with considerable alteration) Babylonian cuneiform. This neo-Elamite cuneiform was very much simpli-fied from the six or seven hundred characters of the Babylonian system: it included a total of 113 symbols, of which over 80 were syllabic.

During all the three thousand or so years during which these various changes and adoptions were taking place, the exquisite Mesopotamian cylinder-seals enjoyed a steady vogue, and they should at least be mentioned in this survey of the history of cuneiform. They have of course been published in great numbers, and little justice can be done to them within the compass of this book.

During most of this period, too, although the Sumerians lost their political independence fifteen hundred years after their first conquest of southern Mesopotamia and although Sumerian had been extinguished as a spoken tongue two or three hundred years later, the Sumerian language continued to be transmitted for ritual, learned and liturgical uses, and made up the basic intellectual and spiritual heritage of the Babylonians, Assyrians, Hittites, and other peoples. It ceased to play this role only when cuneiform itself came to an end.

Around the sixth century B.C., cuneiform was adapted by the Persians to write an Indo-European language. Within a few years, they had simplified it a great deal, creating a phonetic syllabary of forty-one signs which came close to becoming an alphabetic form of writing. But there is a very strong probability that its creation was influenced by the already extant and wide-spread Aramaic alphabet (*see* p. 111 f.).

After its last period of vigour under the Persians, the use of cuneiform became increasingly confined to conservative priests, jurists and astronomers, much like post-medieval Latin. It was first relinquished in private and business letters; examples of such correspondence written in cuneiform disappear completely at the beginning of the fifth century B.C., at which period the spoken Babylonian language also fell into disuse. At the end of the same century, legal contracts and similar documents ceased to be written in cuneiform. A brief renaissance for the script (and for ancient science in general) occurred under the Seleucids, from the third to the first century B.C., but thereafter cuneiform, though it lingered on into the Christian era, moved rapidly to extinction. The last extant record of its use is dated at about A.D. 75. It must have been discontinued after this, for it disappeared completely.

The decipherment of cuneiform – or, more accurately, of the cuneiform scripts – was one of the great achievements of the nineteenth century. In 1800 not a word could be read with certainty; one hundred years later, thousands upon thousands of documents, recording the great and small activities of vast empires, had been deciphered, read, and, to a considerable extent, published.

The Persian cuneiform script, most recent of the major cunei/form writings, was the first to be deciphered. The reason is obvious: it alone was a script of only forty/one characters, representing an Indo/European language. The initial difficul/ties presented by Babylonian cuneiform, with its seven hundred or so characters, and by Sumerian cuneiform, the language of which was completely unknown, were by comparison very great. Nevertheless, even the decipherment of the Persian script was a slow and uncertain affair. After the first major transcrip/tion of cuneiform texts in 1765 (from buildings at Persepolis), nearly half a century passed before G.F.Grotefend, a German high/school teacher, made a major step forward. With little linguistic knowledge, he succeeded, by comparing inscriptions and by a series of brilliant deductions, in assigning correct phonetic values to twelve of the cuneiform characters. Further advances were made by the French orientalist Burnouf and his Norwegian pupil Lassen, who brought comparative linguistics to bear on the problem. The latter proved for the first time that the signs in Persian cuneiform were syllabic and not alphabetic.

But the true 'father' of cuneiform decipherment was Major (later Major General Sir) Henry C. Rawlinson, a British sol/

dier who, while on official duty in Persia, copied, deciphered and translated the complete cuneiform text of the famous tri-lingual inscription at Behistun, which records the achieve-ments of Darius the Great (521–486 B.C.). He published his work on this subject in 1846 and went on subsequently to the successful decipherment of Babylonian cuneiform as well. From this point on it was only a matter of time before all the other major cuneiform writings could also be read.

EGYPTIAN WRITING

Egyptian hieroglyphic writing was, with cuneiform, one of the two most important scripts of the ancient Near East. The quali-fying word 'Egyptian' is now necessary because, within the past half-century, the term 'hieroglyphic' has been applied to other scripts as well, notably the Cretan pictographic, the Hittite and the Mayan. Such application of the term is, however, a minor inaccuracy compounded by a graver one.

HIERO-
GLYPHICS

The term 'hieroglyphic' is a partial transliteration of the Greek *hieroglyphikà grámmata*, derived from *hierós*, 'holy', *gly-pheîn*, 'to carve,' and *grámmata*, 'letters': literally, 'sacred carved letters'. This appellation was founded on the Greek idea that hieroglyphic writing was used principally for religious pur-poses: for monumental inscriptions on temple walls, tombs, sacred monuments, and so forth. This was at least slightly inaccurate since the same kind of writing was used for *painted* inscriptions on wood, earthenware, and other materials besides stone, and for *written* documents on papyrus.

There is, however, an element of truth in the words *hiero-glyphikà grámmata*, as the hieroglyphic script was a monumental writing *par excellence*, equalled only by Roman capitals in this respect. Its *norm* was in its religious function, and the ancient Egyptians themselves, who called it *mdw-ntr*, 'speech of the gods', indicated in this way their continuing conviction of its peculiar sacredness.

To apply the term 'hieroglyphic' to the Cretan pictographic, Hittite and Maya scripts, however, is at best inaccurate and at worst actively misleading. It is meaningless in view of the word's definition, and in the case of the Hittite script implies (even if such implication is unwitting) a direct transmission or influence which never took place.

The earliest extant Egyptian hieroglyphic inscriptions date from the beginning of the third millennium B.C. Until quite recently it was almost universally assumed that the development of Egyptian writing must have followed more or less the same pattern as that of cuneiform: a pictographic script, becoming transitional through the gradual introduction of ideograms and phonograms. But some scholars have begun to question whether this assumption of a gradual development is correct, and have suggested that the script was in fact created artificially at the time of the unification of Egypt under the First Dynasty, by someone already acquainted with the existence of writing. There is at least a possibility that this theory is correct; but the evidence in favour of it is, at the present time, tenuous. On the other hand, no evidence has yet appeared to prove that cunei-form was not, by a few centuries at least, the earlier script.

ORIGINS AND DEVELOP-MENT OF HIERO-GLYPHIC WRITING

Whatever the exact nature of its origins, there is no doubt that during the period of the First Dynasty Egyptian writing reached its full development; and it is now more or less agreed that the rise of this Dynasty took place in the thirtieth or twenty-ninth century B.C. The earliest examples of Egyptian writing yet found are a number of slate palettes from Hierakonpolis in Upper Egypt, fifty miles to the south of Thebes. Of these, the best known is the so-called 'Narmer Palette'; on its two faces we find direct representation of a more or less picto-graphic kind (an Egyptian army marches against its enemies, whose defeat is graphically represented in the same panel;

Plates 9, 10

47

an Egyptian king smites an enemy to his knees), together with a form of semi-phonetic writing used for what are undoubtedly proper names or titles.

Leaving aside the theory that Egyptian writing was wholly artificial in origin, we may say that the Narmer Palette represents a form of writing which has already passed through the stage of simple pictography, and which, in this its earliest appearance, is already a 'transitional' script.

From such scanty evidence as is available, it appears that shortly after the period from which this palette dates a strongly phonetic system of writing had developed in Egypt. Determinatives were introduced to remove the ambiguities of polyphones. And thereafter Egyptian hieroglyphic writing remained fundamentally unchanged for a period of three thousand years.

There were, in all, three classes of hieroglyphic characters: ideograms, phonograms and phonetic complements, and determinatives. The use of ideograms is more or less self-explanatory, especially since such symbols remained clearly pictorial throughout the history of the hieroglyphic script. After the earliest stages of Egyptian writing, however, ideograms seldom appeared in isolation but were almost always accompanied by the phonographic equivalent for the same word, by a phonetic complement, or even by another ideogram serving as a determinative. Much of this repetition and explanation was clearly redundant and various attempts have been made to explain it as having been due to religious conservatism, to the aesthetic sensibilities of the Egyptian scribe, or (and this may be the most likely explanation) to the latter's sense of the mystery of his craft, and his refusal to simplify it in a 'democratic' direction.

The most immediately striking fact about Egyptian writing is that, as in the later Semitic alphabets, only consonants were actually written down: no vowel-sounds were represented. This has nothing to do with the idea which is occasionally expressed, that vowels were 'unimportant' in the Hamito-Semitic lan-

Fig. 8 (and opposite)   Some of the types of palettes used by Egyptian scribes guages, though they played a more subsidiary role than in the Indo-European tongues. In any oral reading from inscriptions or manuscript *all* the unwritten vowels would have had to be pronounced, and pronounced correctly, for the narrative to be understood. It is simply incorrect to assume that a written script whose particular economy is the non-representation of vowels poses any particular difficulty for those accustomed to reading it, and a smpl tst 'f ths srt shld shw ths qut wll.

Egyptian hieroglyphic writing contained approximately seventy-five bi-consonantal phonograms, of which some fifty were commonly used; and, more importantly, twenty-four uni-consonantal signs, later increased to thirty by the addition of homophones, which covered the entire range of consonantal sounds in the Egyptian language.

The existence in Egyptian writing of twenty-four uni-consonantal characters has led a good many persons, including some scholars, to believe that the Egyptians possessed 'the world's earliest alphabet'. Unfortunately, the way in which the Egyptians used their writing indicates how far it was from being an 'alphabet' in any more than the most meaninglessly rhetorical sense. Whereas in a true alphabet each sound is represented by a single constant symbol, Egyptian writing was cluttered with homophones. Whereas the great virtue of an alphabet is its wieldiness and utility, the use of determinatives made the Egyptian script, in comparison with true alphabetic writing, an overwhelmingly cumbersome and complicated affair. And this was true of the script from its origins under the First Dynasty to its end in the reign of Justinian.

Only a single argument therefore remains for the 'alphabetic' nature of Egyptian writing: that it *could* have become alphabetic of its own accord if only matters had been a bit different: if the script had been less scribe-ridden, or if the social structure of ancient Egypt had been less consistently hierarchic. But even this is a fruitless path, for, as we shall see in a moment, popular

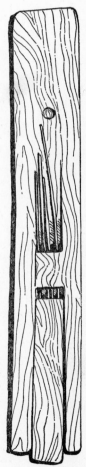

(cursive) scripts *did* arise in Egypt which nevertheless remained, throughout their respective histories, faithful 'transcriptions' of the hieroglyphic script, differing from it in external characteristics only.

All that we have said thus far of the physical nature of the Egyptian script has applied only to the hieroglyphic writing: to those elaborate, monumental characters which were used throughout Egyptian history for sacred inscriptions of all kinds, ritual, royal and funerary. This script was not only chiseled into stone, but drawn and painted as well: yet because of its unique sacredness it never lost its elaboration, its cumbrousness, or its singular beauty.

Plates 11, 12, 13

Plate 14

HIERATIC
WRITING
Plate 15

For the kinds of writing involved in business documents, private letters and literary manuscripts, therefore, it was a very difficult script to use. Moreover, the brush-pen used in drawing on papyrus tended naturally toward a very different kind of line from the thin evenness of chiseled hieroglyphics: towards bolder, more cursive strokes. Hence, there gradually grew up alongside the hieroglyphic script a form of cursive writing which lost more and more of its original pictorial quality. It was used over a period of three thousand years, for profane and sacred purposes of all kinds. By the third century A.D., however, in the time of Clement of Alexandria, it was restricted largely to religious use – employed by the Egyptian priests for transcribing texts of various kinds – and a newer, yet more modified form of cursive writing for every-day use (which we shall discuss below) had been in existence for a millennium. It was at this point that Clement gave the original cursive form its name of *hieratic* (from Greek *hieratikós*, 'sacred' or 'priestly'): a somewhat more misleading repetition of the error made in coining the term *hieroglyphikà grámmata*.

The external changes represented by hieratic writing, which eventually retained only the most rudimentary signs of its pictorial origin, affected the internal nature of the script almost not at all. In practice, the hieratic signs were only transcriptions of the hieroglyphic symbols. The single modification which re-sulted, aside from the minor alteration of the signs themselves, was one which is nearly inevitable in a cursive hand of any sort: many characters were linked together by the sweep of the brush, and ligatured groups of characters were formed. Hieratic was originally written in a vertical direction; subsequently it became horizontal, and was written consistently from right to left.

Hieratic writing of a sort was already in existence under the First Dynasty. As the centuries passed it became increasingly cursive, until, by the seventh century B.C., it had also become rather obscure. By this time, furthermore, it was, in practice, a script of the priestly class: and as a result a new and more modi-fied form of cursive writing came into being for profane use. This script (which was written from right to left) is ordinarily known as demotic, from the Greek *demotikà grámmata* (*démos*, 'people'), a phrase which occurs in Herodotus ii, 36; but Cle-ment of Alexandria called it *grámmata epistolographiká*, 'episto-lary characters'.

The earliest extant demotic document dates from the seventh century B.C., the last from A.D. 476. In its origin, demotic was a direct derivative from hieratic: so that it was, in effect, simply one further 'transcription' of the hieroglyphic script. Like the latter, and like hieratic, it consisted of ideograms, phonograms and determinatives. Externally, however, it was so very cursive a form that there was no longer a trace of the original pictorial symbols from which it was ultimately derived: whole associated groups of hieratic characters were fused, by ligatures, into single

DEMOTIC
WRITING

Fig 9

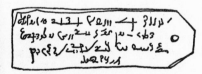

Fig. 9 Wooden label written in de-motic script, from an Egyptian mummy

demotic signs; a compression which makes it today an extremely difficult script to read.

So useful was demotic writing found to be, that from its point
of origin in Lower Egypt it moved on to become the popular
script of the country as a whole; and from its original use for
such every-day purposes as private and commercial correspondence it came to be employed as well for literary compositions,
often of considerable length, and for the copying of ancient
books. Under the Ptolemies demotic came to be considered as
of even greater importance than hieratic, and equal in importance to hieroglyphic writing and Greek. When royal and
priestly decrees were engraved in parallel texts on *stelae*, demotic
was one of the three scripts used – the other two being hieroglyphic and Greek – and occupied the central position, as on
the Rosetta Stone. It continued to be used until the very end of
Egyptian paganism in the fifth century A.D., and handed on to
the Coptic alphabet a number of signs representing Egyptian
sounds which could not be expressed in Greek characters.

It would not be incorrect to say that although, like many
other scripts, Egyptian cursive writing moved steadily in the
direction of convenience and utility, it did this in a purely me-
chanical way; and that its greatest drawback was the conservatism (or self-interest) which prevented any really qualitative
change in the *basis* of the script, as distinguished from its form.

DECIPHER-
MENT OF
EGYPTIAN
WRITING

The history of the decipherment of Egyptian hieroglyphic
writing parallels that of cuneiform in several respects. At the
outset of the nineteenth century not a word could be read. The
efforts of the sixteenth century Italian scholars Valeriano and
Mercati had been in vain; Kircher, the learned Jesuit of the
seventeenth century, had similarly failed; and the eighteenth
century, in the persons of Warburton, de Guignes, and Zoëga,
had produced a number of correct and fruitful guesses as to the
nature of the writing, which, however, laid only the barest
foundations for the work of decipherment.

In 1799, Captain M. Boussard of Napoleon's Army of the Nile found, in the fort of Saint Julien de Rosetta on the mouth of that river, the inscription which we know today as the Rosetta Stone, and which is now in the British Museum. It is a priestly decree in honour of Ptolemy V Epiphanes, drawn up in 197/6 B.C. in two languages and three scripts: parallel Egyptian texts in hieroglyphic (fourteen lines) and demotic (thirty-two lines), and a similar section in Greek (fifty-four lines). The Greek seems, interestingly enough, to have been the original text of the decree, the Egyptian versions being a not-always-literal translation of it.

Given three parallel texts of this kind, one of which posed no linguistic problem at all, real progress began to be made in the work of decipherment – and this despite the fact that the Stone was considerably damaged, especially in its hieroglyphic portion. Considerable advances were made in the decipherment of the demotic, and later of the hieroglyphic as well, by the Swedish orientalist Åkerblad, the French scholar de Sacy, and (most of all) by Dr Thomas Young of Emmanuel College, Cambridge.

The final triumph was reserved, however, for the French Egyptologist Jean François Champollion. Working with all the resources then available – the Stone itself, a knowledge of Coptic (the last stage of the Egyptian language), Åkerblad's decipherment of several phrases in the demotic text, and, what was most important, Young's identification in the hieroglyphic text of several proper names of gods and persons – Champollion, in 1822, published a masterly dissertation on hieroglyphic writing. In this work and in his subsequent researches he laid the foundations of modern Egyptology. Persistent and inevitable scepticism was finally silenced by the successful decipherment of the Decree of Canopus, a *stele* discovered in 1866. And although much remained (indeed, still remains) to be done, the major break-through had been achieved.

CRETAN SCRIPTS

It is worth stating at the outset that in dealing with the his-tory of Cretan writing we are confronted with a good deal of material, the interpretation of which is still in a state of flux. This is only to say that some aspects of our present knowledge of Cretan writings reflect the wider ambiguities of our general knowledge of Aegean history; and that the discoveries and re-search of the past decade, which are in the process of changing our ideas about the latter, cannot fail to modify some of our ideas about the former as well.

At the present time, however, 'flux' is the only proper word for the state of Aegean studies. The discoveries and researches of the period 1952–1956 are still too recent for scholars to have quietly and universally agreed on their significance: a process which cannot be hastened, or conducted with bitterness and rancour. Unfortunately, the latter elements have been intro-duced by recent allegations concerning the methods used by Sir Arthur Evans to substantiate his ideas about Late Minoan Crete. If these allegations prove true in whole or in part, then they will confirm and enhance the general trend of Aegean studies. It is extremely unfortunate that they were initially pre-sented to the public in an over-simplified and overly sensationa-listic form, implying, not an important further modification of our ideas (and one which has been anticipated in various ways for several years) but a revolution. Revolutions are rare in scholarship; this is not one of them.

MINOAN
CULTURE
We do not know to what race the Minoans belonged, what language they spoke, what their origins were; we do not know the details of their history or the names of their rulers. In them-selves such gaps would be a scholarly annoyance; but the results of archaeological excavation on Crete during the past sixty

years, beginning with those of Evans at Knossos, have made this lack of information frustrating in the extreme: for those excavations have uncovered the remains of a brilliant culture, worthy of comparison in its own day with the civilisations of Egypt and Mesopotamia. This culture has traditionally been called *Minoan*, a term coined by Sir Arthur Evans from the name of Minos, legendary king of the so-called (thalasso/cratic) 'Aegean Empire'.

Despite the gaps in our knowledge of the Minoan culture, archaeology has succeeded in establishing, on the basis of *present* knowledge, a fairly exact chronology for the artifacts which have been found on the island. Excavation and exploration at Knossos, Phaistos and Hagia Triada have indicated the existence of a long Neolithic period coinciding at least in part with the Egyptian pre/Dynastic age. This was followed by the Bronze Age civilisation we know as Minoan, which began in approximately the twenty/eighth century B.C.

Evans divided this Minoan epoch into three periods, called, respectively, *Early, Middle* and *Late Minoan:* these three terms being abbreviated for convenience into *E.M., M.M.,* and *L.M.* He then subdivided each period into three phases – *I, II* and *III* – and arrived thus at a total of nine cultural stages altogether.

From *E.M.I* (i.e., from around the twenty/eighth century B.C.) onwards, seal/engraving was practised on Crete, principally in steatite though later in ivory as well. The seals were conical or three/sided and were ordinarily engraved with simple decorative designs, though some were inscribed with crude picture/symbols (including simplified human figures). Some show clear signs of Egyptian influence. Whether these pictorial devices should be considered a true form of writing is an open question.

In *M.M. I* (*c.* 2000–1850 B.C.) these decorative devices were gradually elaborated and the drawings were transformed into true pictograms. Short pictographic inscriptions were cut on

PICTOGRAPH/
IC WRITING

Fig. 10   Cretan pictographic symbols

Figs. 1–4

three- or four-sided seals. Other inscriptions which cannot be classified under the heading of a true script – property marks on vases, and building-stones with masons' marks in a linear form – have been attributed to the same period.

This script of the period *M.M. I* has been designated, correctly, as 'Pictographic Class A'. It is striking that even in this earliest of Cretan writings we find represented the characteristic double-headed axe which seems to have been of particular significance for the Minoan culture.

Fig. 10

In *M.M. II (c.* 1850–1700 B.C.) a more cursive form of writing developed which is known as 'Pictographic Class B'. Besides engravings on seals made of rock crystal, jasper, carnelian and other hard materials, inscriptions in this writing have also been found on tablets of baked clay which may have been used as labels, or as accounts. There were, according to Evans, approximately 135 symbols in use at this stage of the Minoan script, and these included representations of human figures, parts of the body, domestic animals, religious symbols, ships, corn, military equipment, olive sprays, and some purely geometric figures as well. This script (according to Evans) was already partly ideographic and partly phonetic, with a possible use of determinatives as well – in short, a transitional form of writing. A system of numerical notation seems to have been in existence at this stage which was influenced by that of the Egyptians. The direction of writing was from left to right, or in the form known as *boustrophedon* (Greek for 'as the ox plows' – the writing running, in alternate lines, from left to right and from right to left).

Fig. 12

Fig. 11   Minoan Linear A sign list

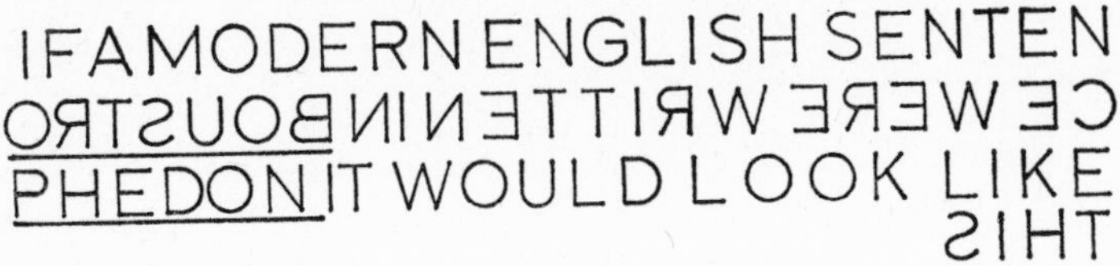

IFAMODERN ENGLISH SENTEN
CE WERE WRITTEN IN BOUSTRO
PHEDON IT WOULD LOOK LIKE
THIS

Fig. 12 Boustrophedon

LINEAR A

Fig. 11

Fig. 13

In *M.M. III* (*a*, until *c.* 1660; *b*, until 1550 B.C.) the first major qualitative change took place in the development of Minoan writing: Pictographic Class B gave way to (or developed into) a more cursive and modified *linear* script which Evans labelled 'Linear Class A', and which is now usually referred to as 'Minoan Linear A'. Inscriptions in this writing (which ran consistently from left to right) have been found engraved on to stone and metal, incised in clay, and written with ink on pottery. The symbols in it number somewhere between seventy-six and ninety, of which between one-third and one-half *only* can be definitely connected with the pictograms of Pictographic Class B. The signs always face away from the beginning of the line. The script may be transitional, but nothing can as yet be said about it with any certainty because it has not been deciphered (despite recent attempts in this direction). According to Evans, it continued in use into *L.M. I* – that is, after the sixteenth century B.C.

Prof. Cyrus Gordon has suggested a decipherment for Linear A, which would indicate that it represents a Semitic language. His decipherment has not, however, been generally accepted. Other scholars – such as Prof. Emilio Peruzzi – have tried to identify the language with an Anatolian Indo-European form of speech.

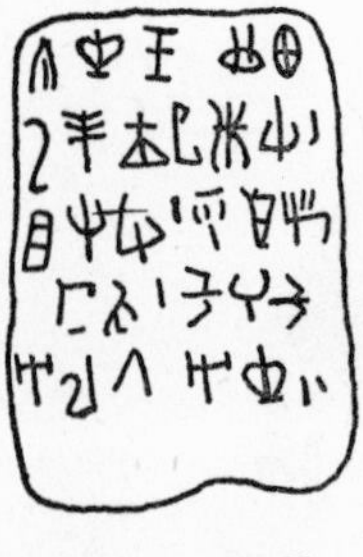

One fact about Linear A stands out which may yet prove to be of great significance: it was not confined to Crete alone, examples having been found on the mainland of Greece (notably at Orchomenos in Boeotia). Why this may be a fact of great significance we shall see in the discussion which follows.

Fig. 13   Tablet inscribed in Minoan Linear A

We come now to the writing which Evans called 'Linear Class B'. So as to shed some light on an issue which has caused a considerable hubbub in recent times, we must digress for a moment in order to give a brief historical sketch of the archaeological exploration of Crete and the Greek mainland.

Plates 17–21
LINEAR B

In the history of that exploration, there have been several major discoveries each of which has, in turn, necessitated major revisions in our traditional conceptions of pre-Classical Greek and Aegean history. The first of these was Schliemann's historic work of excavation at Mycenae, in the late nineteenth century: for this revealed the remains of a great and powerful culture, since labelled Mycenaean, which came into existence on the mainland of Greece long before the Classical period, and before the Greek 'Dark Age' out of which the Classical period is traditionally thought to have arisen.

The second great discovery was that made by Sir Arthur Evans at Knossos: for his exacavations there revealed, as has been mentioned, a great civilisation hitherto unknown. They took place in the period 1900–1905; and it was in 1900 that he first came upon clay tablets inscribed in Linear B.

For the later history of the Minoan civilisation, and its relations with Mycenae, Evans postulated (and defended) roughly the following picture. Schliemann's Mycenae was fundamentally a 'transmarine offshoot' from the 'Minoan stock'. When, at the end of *L.M. II*, in about 1400 B.C., the great Cretan civilisation was suddenly brought to an end and the great palace at Knossos destroyed, the Mycenaean mainlanders at last came into their own and proceeded to establish their hegemony over the Aegean. The *L.M. III* period on Crete was one of decadence and general dilapidation. The Mycenaeans, though they established themselves on Cyprus, left Crete untouched. With the fall of the true Minoan civilisation Linear B came to an end as well, the 'squatters' who subsequently occupied the site of Knossos being illiterate.

With some sporadic opposition or attempts at modification, this picture was generally accepted.

In 1939, a thirteenth-century Mycenaean palace was unearthed at Pylos in the south-western Peloponnese, which yielded six hundred clay tablets bearing a form of writing that was clearly a close variant of Linear B. This in itself was startling: it disposed once and for all of the idea that such scattered examples of Linear B as had hitherto been found on the mainland had simply been carried there from Crete; and of the alternative view that, although rudimentary inscriptions in Linear B may have been written on the mainland, nothing of a more lengthy or systematic nature was produced outside of Crete itself.

DECIPHER-
MENT OF
LINEAR B

But this was only the beginning. As a result of the war and other delays, the tablets found at Pylos were not published until 1951. One year later the late Michael Ventris announced his decipherment of Linear B. And this constituted the third great discovery after Schliemann and Evans: because the language of Linear B was Greek.

The revolutionary effects of this decipherment can be succinctly stated. It now seems certain that the Mycenaeans were in fact Greeks, linguistically related to the Arcadians. None of the Linear B documents are literary in character; but the short economic and military 'account books' that have been found have immeasurably extended our knowledge of Mycenaean civilisation, and have already begun to cast new light on Homer (see especially Denys Page's *History and the Homeric Iliad*).

Thus at one stroke what is practically a revolution has taken place in Greek studies. The prehistoric period of the Middle and Late Bronze Ages on the mainland (Middle and Late Helladic) must now be recognised as Hellenic; we cannot include Crete, because we cannot yet read the Minoan Linear A script, which represents a different language from the Linear B script, and thus the Minoan culture cannot be called Hellenic. We must in future differentiate between the Linear A *Minoan* script and the Linear B *Mycenaean* script, for the latter is far commoner on the Mainland, where it is found from Orchomenos in the north to Pylos in the south, than it is in Crete. (Foreword by A. J. B. Wace to *Documents in Mycenaean Greek*)

Allowing for a degree of overstatement and enthusiasm, we must say that the picture presented by Wace is substantially correct.

In 1952–4, further Mycenaean tablets in Linear B were unearthed at Pylos and Mycenae. Jars with Linear B inscriptions have been found at four sites apart from those that have yielded tablets. Altogether more Linear B inscriptions have now been found on the mainland than on Crete itself: a truly momentous change from the period of Evans's excavations.

What of the effect of this discovery on Minoan, as distinguished from mainland, studies? The key fact here is that the Linear B documents found on Crete seem to be as much Greek as those found on the mainland. If the recent allegations concerning Sir Arthur Evans's findings at Knossos prove true, then they may safely be called Mycenaean as well.

Evans's views on the history of Late Minoan Crete have already been mentioned. The revised view would be along the following lines. Some time around 1400 B.C., the Cretan civilisation was taken over by the Mycenaean Greeks in the course of their expansion across the Aegean: it was not destroyed. Under its new rulers the Minoan culture continued virtually unchanged until its final destruction, possibly at the hands of the Dorian Greeks, in about 1100 B.C. The Mycenaeans introduced into Crete their own script, Linear B: a form of writing which they may originally have derived from the Minoan Linear A. Speculative as this outline is, it represents the *general* direction in which the history of the Aegean and of pre-Classical Greece has begun to move.

A word should be said about the physical nature of the Linear B script. It consists of some eighty-nine characters, of which forty-eight can be traced back to Linear A. Like the latter, it is a cursive form of writing, running from left to right; but its system of numeration is considerably different from that of Class A in the treatment of fractional quantities, a fact which perhaps substantiates its 'artificial' origins (that is, its conscious adaptation to the Greek language). Such a change would have caused immense difficulties for commerce and record-keeping of all kinds wherever a fully-developed form of writing was already in existence. Unlike Linear A, the lines of writing on the Linear B tablets are separated by guide lines.

ETEO-
CRETAN

Two other Cretan scripts which have no ascertainable relation to either the Minoan or Mycenaean cultures remain to be mentioned. The first of these is represented by the so-called 'eteo-Cretan' inscriptions found at Praïsos, written in an early form of the Greek alphabet but in an unknown language.

PHAISTOS
DISC
Plate 22

The second is that of the Phaistos Disc, an irregularly circular terra-cotta tablet, between six and seven inches in diameter, which is not only the single most remarkable inscription found on Crete, but also an example of a rudimentary form of printing all the more remarkable for its lack of progeny. It dates from approximately 1700 B.C. Each of the disc's two faces is divided by a spiral line into five coils. Along these coils, characters were impressed or printed by means of separate stamps, and were divided into groups of between two and seven symbols by vertical lines. The characters are highly pictorial, but (except for a few casual resemblances) show no affinity with Cretan pictograms. There are altogether, on both faces of the tablet, 241 symbols: 123 on one face, separated into thirty/one groups; and 118 on the other, in thirty groups. The characters include a galley, hatchet, house, carpenter's square, eagle, rosette and vase; the head of a man wearing a plumed head/dress (very frequently repeated); and a very animated figure of a man walking. The direction of the writing is from right to left, human and animal figures always facing left.

A number of conjectural foreign points of origin have been suggested for the Phaistos Disc, including the south/west coast of Asia Minor, North Africa and Philistia. But since no form of writing even remotely analogous has been found anywhere outside of Crete, we cannot exclude the possibility of its having had an indigenous Cretan origin.

INDUS VALLEY SCRIPT

Until well into the twentieth century the common assumption about civilisation in India was that none existed until the Indo/Aryan invasion of the second millennium B.C. Several decades of excavation, exploration and study have by now conclusively shattered this idea, and have uncovered, in the general area of the Indus Valley, the remains of a considerable civilisation dating to the beginning or middle of the third millennium B.C.

The Indus Valley civilisation may be divided into the urban Harappa Culture on the one hand, and a number of peasant cultures on the other. Excavation of the latter has only really begun since 1931, and has still not proceeded in a full or con/clusive fashion: so that the remarks which follow must be taken as dealing primarily with the Harappa Culture. We must keep in mind the possibility that further excavation and study will disclose a prehistoric civilisation in India far more extensive than we can yet even infer.

The urban centres of the Harappa Culture, or at least those which have been excavated hitherto, were the great cities of Harappa and Mohenjo/daro, and some smaller towns and

*Fig. 14 Seal in-
scriptions in the
Indus Valley
script*

villages in what is today southern Sind. Excavations at these sites have disclosed regular and well-planned streets running along the major points of the compass, excellent drainage and water-supply, public baths (perhaps for ritual purposes of some kind), and other indications of a careful system of town-planning. Even more striking as evidence of the degree of civilisation attained by the Harappa people was the discovery of spacious and well-equipped private houses built of baked brick and supplied with such conveniences as wells, bath-rooms, and other excellent sanitary arrangements. In these dwellings were found sculptures in alabaster and marble, many clay and faience figurines, tools of stone, copper and bronze, stamp-seals of faience (which may have been used as amulets) with animal figures in relief (generally a bull, rhinoceros or elephant), personal ornaments of all kinds, and elaborately carved stone and ivory seals inscribed with what we now refer to as the Indus Valley Script.

All the evidence hitherto found has substantiated the picture of the Harappa Culture as one of a flourishing economy based on agriculture and husbandry, carrying on commerce by land and sea, and practising the manufacture of cotton cloth as well.

This much has been discovered: but the gaps in our knowledge of the Indus Valley civilisation remain overwhelmingly large. Measurement of skeletal remains has indicated that its founders were of the Mediterranean type, and hence probably immigrants from the west. But we do not know the name of this people, what language they spoke, or their place of origin. We do not know whether they brought their civilisation with them, or whether this was importantly influenced by whatever indigenous culture they found in India when they arrived. Nor has there been found any conclusive evidence to suggest a link between the Indus Valley civilisation and the Indo-Aryan culture which appeared in India a millennium or more later.

The most striking characteristic of the Harappa Culture was

its use of an indigenous script. This has been found on the
seals already mentioned (these being ordinarily flat, and very occasionally cylindrical), and on pottery of various kinds. The script (all attempts at the decipherment of which have hitherto failed) is made up of approximately three hundred characters – the estimates of various scholars range from 253 to 396. This is too large a number for an alphabetic or syllabic script, and too small for one which is simply ideographic: so that it is probable that the Indus Valley Script was a transitional form of writing.

The symbols retain clear signs of their pictorial origins, though they are strongly stylised. The seal-inscriptions, eight hundred examples of which have been found, seem to represent proper names; but this does not rule out the possibility that more perishable materials were employed in the Harappa Culture for longer, or more literary, documents.

It is impossible to judge, at the present time, whether the Indus Valley Script was indigenous in origin or imported from elsewhere. There are certain resemblances to the earliest form of the cuneiform script (that is, cuneiform in its pictographic stage), a fact which may be explained in one of two ways: either the Indus Valley Script was derived from a very early form of writing, at present unknown, which was also the common ancestor of Sumerian cuneiform and (perhaps) of proto-Elamite; or all three of these scripts were local creations, one of which (perhaps the basic form of either cuneiform or proto-Elamite) inspired the invention of the other two *indirectly*, through a knowledge of its existence (a process of the kind which is now known as 'idea-diffusion').

On the question of the supposed influence of the Indus Valley Script on other, later, forms of writing one can only render a verdict of *not proven*. It has been suggested (and accepted by a number of scholars) that it has some connection with the *Brahmi* writing, the prototype of nearly all later Indian scripts. But there is at the present time no evidence that the

Indus Valley Script continued in existence between the last centuries of the third millennium and the first half of the first millennium B.C.; there are no traces of it in the most ancient Indian literature; and, since it has not been deciphered, there is no evidence for any linguistic continuity which would add substance to this hypothesis. Most of the other 'influences' which have been suggested – such as a connection with the Easter Island writing, or with the North Semitic alphabet – are even less tenable than this, relying for the most part on external and superficial resemblances.

HITTITE SCRIPTS

We should make it clear at the outset that the term 'Hittite' is not equivalent to the terms 'Egyptian' or 'Assyrian': for the Hittites as we know them, the Hittites who created a civilisation comparable in degree of power and advancement to those of the Egyptians, Babylonians and Assyrians, were in fact a mixture of peoples of different ethnic and linguistic affinities.

In the middle of the third millennium B.C., eastern Asia Minor was peopled by a racial stock of the Armenoid type: dark, thickset men with backwardsloping foreheads, large aquiline noses, and slightly receding chins. They spoke a nonIndoEuropean language and lived in citystates, one of which, Hatti (or Khatti), succeeded after a prolonged struggle in gaining supremacy over the others. From its name has been derived the generally accepted modern term for this indigenous group, the Hattic people.

During the last centuries of the third millennium B.C. there occurred throughout western Asia an invasion of IndoEuropean peoples, one group of which overcame the Hattic people of Asia Minor. These IndoEuropeans, whether from tolerance or fear, did not hold aloof from the people they had conquered but intermixed freely with them. Hence, in the new ('Hittite')

group which this interbreeding produced, the Armenoid Hattic type was once again predominant, while Hattic speech
strongly influenced the Indo-European tongue of the new-
comers. The older ethnic name (Hebrew *Hittim*, Egyptian
Kheta, and possibly Homeric *Keteioi*) continued to be used
abroad to describe the people as a whole.

They soon constituted an empire. The city of Hatti, whose
name was altered to Hattushash (modern Boghazköy), became the capital of a strong kingdom which succeeded in over-
throwing the Hammurabi dynasty of Babylonia. After an
eclipse of fortune in the sixteenth and fifteenth centuries B.C.
there occurred the rise of the Hittite New Empire, which, from
the fourteenth to the end of the thirteenth century, had no rival
for supremacy on its eastern and south-eastern borders, and was
in no wise inferior to the empire of the Egyptians. It came to an
end in the beginning of the twelfth century B.C., overthrown
by the invaders known as the 'Sea-Peoples'. The Hittite political and cultural centre was transferred to northern Syria, where
small Hittite states arose, the most important of which was
Carchemish. In the eighth century B.C. these kingdoms were
conquered by the Assyrians, Carchemish falling to Sargon II
in the year 717 B.C.

The earliest form of Hittite writing was an adaptation of
Babylonian cuneiform to the basically Indo-European Hittite
language. Examples of this writing have been found in the
Hittite royal archives at Hattushash (the principal source for all
study of Hittite history and civilisation). Although it continued
to be written until after 1200 B.C., it seems never to have been
in use beyond the area around Hattushash itself. Its most not-
able trait is a certain complexity, since it often carried over intact
Babylonian and even Sumerian linguistic usages. The Hittites,
however, 'greatly reduced the number of signs in common use,
and their script is further simplified by their introduction of the
practice of separating their words.' (Gurney)

HITTITE
CUNEIFORM
WRITING

Sometime around 1500 B.C., when this Hittite cuneiform had long been in use, there came into being the form of writing usually referred to as Hittite 'hieroglyphic' – an unfortunate name which we shall have to use in this discussion. Comparatively few of the extant inscriptions in this script have hitherto been found in the territory of the Hittite empire proper, the greater number dating from the period of the Syrian Hittite states (and especially from the tenth to the eighth century B.C.).

The origins of Hittite hieroglyphic writing remain obscure, but there are external similarities to Cretan pictographic writing which indicate, not a direct borrowing of any kind, but some form of idea-diffusion.

Fig. 15 Part of a late and stylised inscription in Hittite hieroglyphic writing (c. 600 B.C.) from Bulgar Dagh (Bulgarmaden)

The origin of the script can be dated at approximately 1500 B.C.; the last examples of it at *c.* 600 B.C. The earliest versions are highly pictorial, a quality which was to some extent preserved throughout the history of the script, even in the more cursive forms of its last period. The writing begins at the top right-hand side of whatever surface was used and generally moves thereafter in *boustrophedon* – though occasionally the direction of writing is simply from left to right, or from right to left. There are 220 characters in the script; they always face towards the beginning of the line. Sixty of the symbols represent syllabic (uni-consonantal) phonograms; the remainder are ideograms, some of them also used as determinatives.

Most of the extant Hittite hieroglyphic inscriptions are engraved on stone monuments or on rocks, and occasionally such inscriptions were chiseled in relief, the background, and not Plate 24 the characters themselves, being hollowed out – an unusual technique which produced some of the most beautiful of the Hittite inscriptions. Sometimes the surface used was lead, sometimes clay, while the famous Tarkondemos seal is in silver.

Thanks to the researches of a great number of modern scholars, and the discovery of the Karatepe Phoenician-Hittite bilingual inscription, Hittite hieroglyphic writing can today be read with a fair degree of certainty: disputes on particular points continue, but there is increasing agreement on the main points of decipherment.

Chapter III

The Far East

CHINESE WRITING

THE CHINESE SCRIPT, an analytic system of writing about or nearly four thousand years old, is today employed by a nation comprising approximately a quarter of the world's population, and extending over an area larger than the entire continent of Europe. Although it has had a longer span of existence than any other extant script, its internal development has been practically non-existent: such changes as have taken place in Chinese writing have been technical and external – calligraphic changes, but not alterations in basic structure.

EARLIEST
CHINESE
WRITING

Plate 25

The origins of Chinese writing remain obscure. The earliest documents we know of, differing only externally from the Chinese script of the twentieth century, date from the middle of the second millennium B.C. They comprise oracle texts on animal bones and tortoise shells (the so-called 'Honan bones'), and short inscriptions on bronze vessels, weapons, pottery and jade. Some of these inscriptions contain only a character or two, representing proper names and religious functions. The oracle texts – generally believed to be *responsa* given by royal diviners to private individuals who sought their aid – are a bit more lengthy.

Although even Chinese palaeographers could make out no more than a word or two of the oracle texts when they were first discovered in 1899, they have since been (to a good extent) deciphered, largely through the work of Chinese scholars; a feat which deserves to rank with the decipherment of the Egyptian hieroglyphics and the cuneiform scripts.

At this earliest-known stage of its development, the Chinese script contained no more than 2,500 or 3,000 characters – there is still some uncertainty, in the reading of the Honan bones, as to the differentiation between separate symbols and mere variants of a symbol – the majority of which still show clear signs of their pictorial origin. Approximately six hundred of these have been identified with certainty, and as a result the inscriptions can be adequately understood.

In these earliest specimens of the script, Chinese writing is already a transitional form: the increment of phonograms had begun. Ordinarily this fact would argue for the script's having previously undergone a long period of development, through pictographic and ideographic stages of considerable length. The lack of evidence for any earlier stage of this kind raises three possibilities: (1) either the earlier writing was done on such perishable materials as wood or bamboo, none of which could have survived in the damp Chinese climate; or (2) Chinese was an artificially-created script, perhaps distantly influenced by early cuneiform through 'idea diffusion' (in which case it would have been *invented* as a transitional script); or (3) an earlier form of the writing still awaits discovery. In dealing with these possibilities we must remember that all we know of Chinese history before approximately 800 B.C. is highly uncertain and conjectural; and all that can be said with any certainty today is that no evidence has hitherto appeared to suggest that Chinese writing originated anywhere outside of China itself.

From the middle of the second millennium B.C. until the second century A.D., when they were defined by Hsü Shên, the principles of the construction of the Chinese script remained the same. In form, however, the script changed a good deal. The earliest written or painted inscriptions were drawn with a stylus of bamboo or metal, with which lines and curves of unvarying thickness could easily be traced. (Engraving was done with bronze knives.) Some time in or before the third century B.C., there was invented the *pi*, the famous Chinese writing brush made of elastic hair which so enormously in-

DEVELOP-
MENT OF
CHINESE
WRITING

fluenced the subsequent evolution of the script. Painted in a dark varnish, the characters now tended increasingly to lose both their rounded curves and their likeness to the ideograms from which they had ultimately sprung: a process analogous, in many ways, to the development of Egyptian demotic writing out of the hieroglyphic and hieratic scripts. With the invention of paper in A.D. 105 Chinese writing began to take on the appearance so familiar today: flowing strokes of varying thick-ness, straight or with gentle curves. In the fourth century A.D. the classical Chinese script, *k'ai shu*, was invented. Many cur-sive and ornamental scripts have appeared since that time, but *k'ai shu* has remained the norm.

The Chinese script was and is written vertically, from top to bottom, beginning on the right-hand side of the writing surface and (when in bound form) on what we ordinarily regard as the last page of a book.

Thus far, our discussion has been concerned largely with the physical nature of Chinese writing: and indeed this is in its own right a very important subject, since among the Chinese calligraphy has traditionally been an art higher in status than even landscape painting; an art demanding great patience, training and skill. But we must now turn our attention to the script as a representation of language. As we shall see, the history of the script in this respect is inseparably bound up with a scholarly tradition at least three thousand years old.

In its earliest period, the then very limited number of pho-netic characters in Chinese writing represented the spoken Chinese language of that time. That language was then, and is now, basically monosyllabic; with the result that the same monosyllable has often to serve as a spoken representation for a great many different things and meanings. This limitation has traditionally been overcome, and the Chinese language has been made wieldy and flexible, by the use of characteristic variations in *tone:* so that by pronouncing a particular mono-

Fig. 16
Plate 26

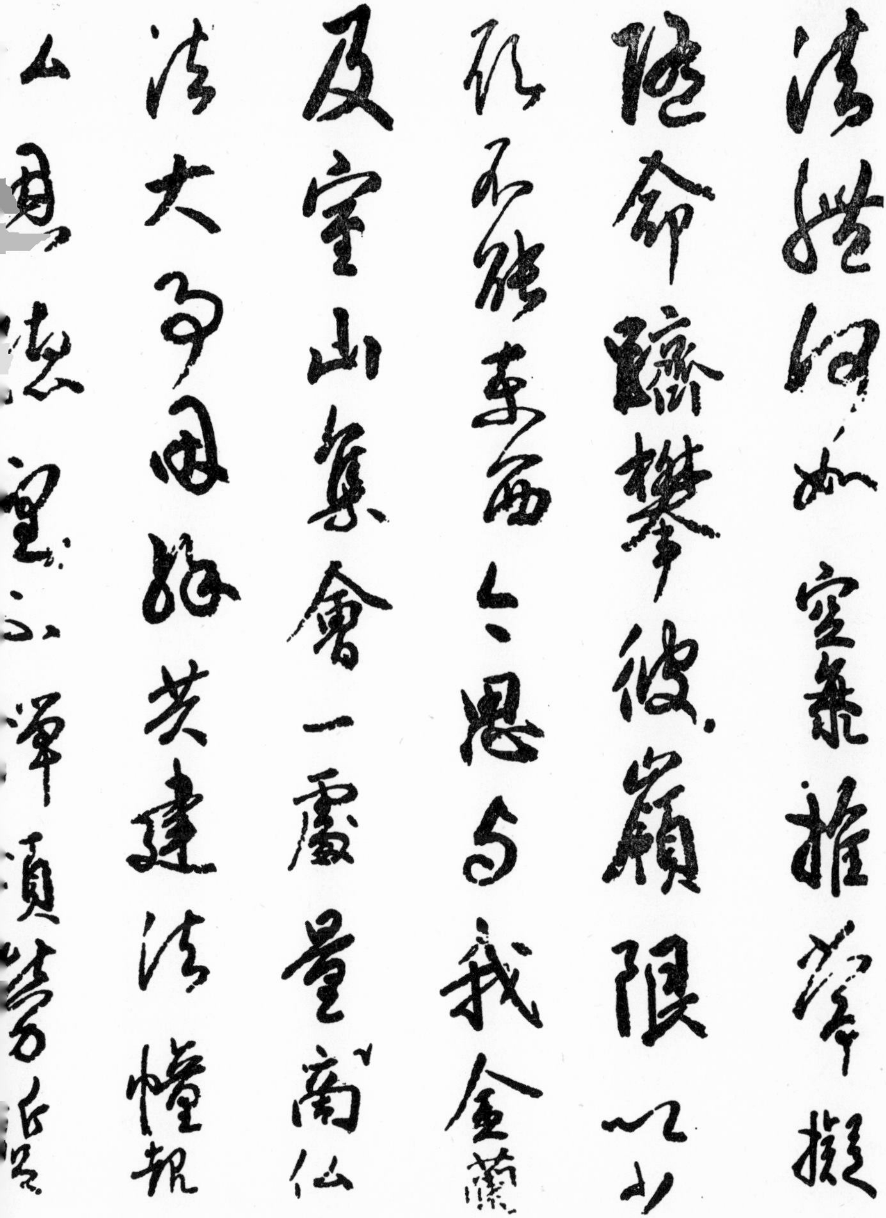

Fig. 16   Chinese calligraphy: Kukai (A.D. 778–835) from a Buddhist text by Fushinjo

syllable in a rising, falling or otherwise varied pithc, one re-duces its range of meaning to perhaps ten or twenty possible alternatives, while the 'context of situation' does the rest. An-other device which has also facilitated understanding is the use of 'synonym-compounds' – pairs of words with similar meanings, one of which helps to make the other recognisable.

Something like this situation was already well in existence when the earliest-known inscriptions were written, and its effects on the script were to be profound: a considerable (in-deed, nearly absolute) barrier was put in the way of Chinese writing ever becoming a simple phonetic script.

The use of ideograms posed no problem, of course, since these tend to be self-explanatory. Moreover, ideographic com-binations of the sort in which Chinese writing is very rich began to be used at an early period: *e.g.* the character repre-senting 'woman', reproduced twice, stands for the word 'quarrel' (*wân*); 'to hear' + 'door' = 'to listen'; 'man' + 'word' = 'sincere' or 'true'; and so forth. Other methods were also found to broaden, modify and extend the meanings of different ideograms, such as the inversion or tilting of individual charac-ters, and the use of associational compounds of various kinds.

HSING-
SHÊNG

The use of phonograms – and as we have seen, they were already used in the earliest inscriptions known to us – intro-duced many grave difficulties. When a single monosyllabic word could (without inflection) be taken to stand for a dozen or more different meanings, then to write it as a simple phono-gram was to give the reader nothing but the 'context of situa-tion' to assist him in selecting the meaning intended at a parti-cular point. Despite this handicap, considerable use was made of pure phonograms, especially before the first millennium A.D. But inevitably there was introduced the script-form known to Chinese lexicographers as *hsing shêng*, 'to harmonise sound': what we could call phonetic compounds. By the tenth century A.D., it had come to constitute the most important element in the Chinese script, totalling 7,697 out of 10,516 characters; while today *hsing shêng* comprises nine-tenths of all the symbols in Chinese writing. As this development implies, it was *hsing shêng* which made it possible to increase (even to excess) the number of characters in the Chinese script, and at the same time to eliminate the more obvious ambiguities.

Each of the characters in *hsing shêng* is a compound of two symbols, one acting as a phonetic element and the other as a determinative (or 'radical'). Let us take, for example, the word *k'o*, 'river'. The first element of this compound is the symbol for *kò*, 'fruit' (originally a picture of a cluster of fruit on a tree). This symbol has no association with the *meaning* of the compound, but indicates what the final pronunciation is to be like. To it is added the determinative symbol – in this case, the character *shui*, 'water'. Thus, someone not quite proficient in the reading of Chinese would have to go through the following train of associations: (1) the word intended at this point sounds roughly like *kò*; (2) it has some essential connection with the general concept 'water'; (3) the word is k'o, 'river'.

Two other examples of *hsing shêng* are: *kûng* ('handiwork')+ *hsin* ('heart') = *k'ûng* ('impatience'); and *kûng* + *yên* ('words') = *kûng* ('quarrel').

With the development of *hsing shêng*, and the spread of the knowledge of writing over all the immense territory of China, there began an excessive multiplication of symbols in the script. Many useless and confusing abbreviations and compounds came into use, and outright errors of various kinds were transmitted by ignorant scribes. As a result Chinese scholars began, well before the first century A.D., to attempt some systematisation of the Chinese script, expending upon this effort considerable labour and ingenuity. Around the eleventh century B.C. there appeared the earliest attempt at classification, called *Erh ya*: a collection of terms arranged in nineteen categories. At the end of the third century B.C., Li

Ssŭ, a minister of the first Ch'in emperor, compiled an official catalogue of the Chinese script, *San ts'ang*, in which he listed a total of 3,300 characters.

Four centuries later, in the second century A.D., Hsü Shên published the lexicon *Shuo wên chieh tzŭ* ('An Explanation of Ancient Figures and Analysis of Compound Characters'). This work, which amended the catalogue of Li Ssŭ, has not survived in its original form, but it became the basis for all subsequent study and classification of Chinese writing. According to W. P. Yetts, Hsü Shên 'was chiefly concerned with the form of characters and their origins, though he added brief explanations of the meanings. His sources were the surviving classics, the writings of his predecessors, and inscriptions on bronze and stone'.

YÜN FU

In the sixth century A.D. Chinese scholars began to compile the phonetic dictionaries, *yün fu*, in which words were classified according to their sound or tone; this mode of distinction being, as we have seen, the defining characteristic of the Chinese language in all its dialects and throughout its history. The first of these, *Yü p'ien*, was published in A.D. 543; it was also the earliest dictionary to employ the *fan ch'ieh* system, which, in the twentieth century, became the basis of an attempt to simplify the Chinese script in the direction of a syllabary. Essentially, this system reduces the number of symbols in the script by employing two syllables to express a third for which no phonetic representation exists. Thus, the syllable *yu* may be written, in *fan ch'ieh*, as *yi-u;* the syllable *ming* as *mi-eng;* and so forth. In its earliest appearances, *fan ch'ieh* was employed only sporadically, and was used to elucidate the pronunciation and reading of especially obscure characters.

In A.D. 601 the *Ch'ieh yün*, a phonetic dictionary of northern China, was published. It was enlarged one hundred and fifty years later under the title *T'ang yün*, and this in turn was included in a compilation made in 986 by an imperial commission under Hsü Hsüan. The latter was also called *Shuo wên chieh tzŭ*, reproducing the title of Hsü Shên's influential lexicon of the second century. It was in turn revised by another imperial commission in 1011; and a series of revisions and additions followed until the publication by the emperor K'ang Hsi (1662–1722) of his great dictionary of the Chinese language. In this work, the total number of characters in the Chinese script – approximately 2,500 in the second millenium B.C., 3,300 in the third century B.C., and 10,516 in the tenth century A.D. – was listed as 44,449. By now, the compound *hsing shêng* had become the predominant element in the script, and so K'ang Hsi arranged this immense number of characters under 214 determinatives, further classification in each category being made according to the number of strokes in the phonetic element of the compound. Over thirty thousand of the words listed in K'ang Hsi's lexicon were either out of date, doubles (i.e. different ways of writing the same word), or faulty.

At the present time there remain in current use in the Chinese script approximately 8,000 characters. But the difficulties of continuing to use a transitional script in the twentieth century, in the face of the nearly universal adoption and adaptation of alphabetic writing, have become increasingly apparent, and have already led to important modifications. Thus, a kind of 'basic' Chinese has grown up for use in popular literature which includes a maximum of between 600 and 1,000 characters. Even this simplification has not made the script a really wieldy one, and for the past decade or so the Communist Chinese government has undertaken a systematic revision of the script in the direction of an alphabet, and of some form of Romanisation. Nothing can yet be said about the realisation of this project. Unsuccessful experiments have previously been made in the adoption of an alphabetic form of writing for the Chinese language. If the present systematic reform is put into effect, it will represent the first major qualitative change which

SIMPLIFI-
CATION

has ever occurred in the recorded history of the Chinese writing.

The problem of the adaptation of Chinese to the modern world is complicated by its extreme paucity of grammatical structure: there is, strictly speaking, no Chinese grammar apart from syntax, since the same word may be used as a verb, a noun or an adjective, its precise usage at any point being determined only by its place in the sentence. It is further complicated by the existence of dialects so varied that scholars from one region of China might find the speech of scholars from another region quite incomprehensible: though they could communicate with ease in writing. In recent times, however, a modernised educational system has caused the Mandarin dialect to acquire a more or less 'official' standing, and its establishment throughout the country will almost certainly be hastened and intensified by the introduction and spread in rural areas of such forms of mass communication as radio, television and the cinema.

NON-CHINESE SCRIPTS OF CHINA

The Chinese script is, as we have mentioned, the only transitional form of writing which is still a major instrument of communication in its own right. Indeed, assuming that the transition to an alphabetic form is *not* made, its importance may very well increase as the Chinese constitute an ever-larger percentage of the world's total population.

This makes it all the more interesting that within the borders of China there should have existed in the past and lingered on into modern times a number of non-Chinese peoples with their own languages and scripts. At one time the non-Chinese regions were truly immense, and Chinese control of them was less *de facto* than *de jure*. These peoples constituted a perpetual threat or annoyance; and when hostilities were in a latent stage, 'pacification' often took the form of recognising their indigenous chieftains as Chinese officials, with the addition of official Chinese names to their own titles.

The broken non-Chinese tribes still in existence within and without the borders of China proper are the last remnants of these peoples. Nowadays they remain in bulk and unabsorbed only in the southwestern provinces of China: and although little is any longer heard of them, there can be no doubt that under a government which puts a powerful stress on unity and homogeneity their life-spans as independent or even semi-independent tribes are nearly at an end.

One of these peoples are the Lo-Lo, who are found in north-ern Indo-China as well and who have received much study at the hands of French missionaries. Lo-lo is actually a group of languages spoken by about 1,800,000 people in Yün-nan, Hsi-kang and Sze-chwan, and the nearly inacessible Mt Liang area between these provinces.

The existence of a Lo-lo script was first noted by Europeans in the seventies of the last century. In 1886, F. S. A. Bourne obtained from an aged Lo-lo a list of all the characters he could remember – the script by this time having fallen into disuse – and this method produced a total of 376. According to later scholars, however, the Lo-lo writing contained some three thousand symbols. There are in existence many Lo-lo manu-scripts, some of which are finely illustrated. The characters are largely ideographic, with some phonograms, and they consist to a good extent of adaptations, contractions and combinations of Chinese signs.

The Lo-lo script was by no means unitary. There are local varieties which may be placed in two principal groupings, according to the direction in which they are intended to be read. The Ta Liang-shan tribes (Mt Liang area) used a ho-rizontal script running from right to left; other tribes, prob-ably through Chinese influence, used principally a vertical script: the columns ran, however, from left to right.

Very little is known of the origins or early development of Lo⁄lo writing. An inscription found at Tsan⁄tsin⁄gay, near Lu⁄ch'üan⁄hsien, has been attributed to A.D. 1533. A theory has been put forward suggesting that Lo⁄lo writing is a link between the scripts of India, Indonesia and Indo⁄China, and those of Korea and Japan. Thus far, however, no proof has been found to substantiate this idea.

NA⁄KHI
SCRIPT

The proper home of the Na⁄khi people, who are linguistical⁄ly related to the Lo⁄lo, is the valley of the Mekong River im⁄mediately to the east of upper Burma, and the valley of the Yang⁄tse in the vicinity of Li⁄kiang (north⁄western Yün⁄nan). They are also scattered throughout the other provinces of south⁄western China. The Chinese name for the Na⁄khi, 'Mo⁄so', has an insulting meaning ('miserable'); Na⁄khi or Na⁄shi is the indigenous name.

Mention of the Na⁄khi is made several times in Chinese historical sources, the first such record occurring in the eighth century A.D. In the second half of the thirteenth century they became a vassal state of Kublai Khan, and in later periods they recognised what was to them the shadowy authority of China. They finally lost their independence to China around 1725, though some tribes were still living under the rule of their own chieftains in recent years.

Like Lo⁄lo writing, the Na⁄khi script raises many prob⁄lems. It was discovered in the middle of the last century, but its origins remain unknown, or at least uncertain. According to Père Desgodins, the actual discoverer, it has not had an extensive history of any kind, having been created by the *tombas* (or medicine men), in comparatively recent times. Later scho⁄lars have tentatively disagreed with this theory, pointing out that this crude, highly pictorial script retains characteristics of an early stage of pictography long ago superseded in adjacent areas. That it is in fact an early and unusual 'survival' has not, however, been conclusively proven.

Today, the Na-khi script has fallen into disuse. The southern Na-khi employ Chinese characters, while those of the north have until quite recently used the Tibetan alphabet.

Many illustrated Na-khi manuscript have been preserved, including some at the John Rylands Library in Manchester. They are largely in the form of little books about three inches high and ten inches wide. The leaves are made of a thick, rough paper of uneven texture.

The Man linguistic group of peoples (Chinese: *Man* = 'southern barbarian') extends over south-western China, what was formerly Indo-China, and Burma, the chief groups in it being the Miao (or Miao-tzu) and the Yao.

The Miao are a mountain people found today in south-western China (though at one time they occupied a portion of central China as well), northern Burma, and northern Indo-China. They number approximately 2,000,000 in China alone and are subdivided into about seventy tribes. Some of these still enjoyed a measure of autonomy in recent times.

The script of the Miao was an ideographic form of writing of the kind sometimes designated as 'cryptic': that is, it was essentially a private code, the key to which was jealously guarded from outsiders and particularly from foreigners. As a result, American and English missionaries preaching the Gospel to illiterate Miao mountaineers in the late nineteenth century remained quite unaware of the fact that an indigenous script existed, and proceeded to invent a wholly new system of writing for those whom they attempted to convert. The new script was a syllabary, consisting of extremely simple geometrical symbols, and was completed in 1904. According to the missionaries themselves, the success of their invention was 'immediate and phenomenal'. The first shipment of the Gospels printed in the new script to reach Yünnan-fu, a provincial capital of the Miao, 'had been sold within two hours, although the consignment made up twenty-nine horse-loads.'

The new system of writing was subsequently adapted, in the same region, to a variety of other non⁄Chinese dialects.

The Yao, numbering only about 30,000, live principally in the south⁄western portions of the Chinese provinces of Kwan⁄ tung and Kwang⁄si, though a few are found in upper Burma, and to the east of the Mekong River. Like that of the Miao, their writing is a cryptic ideographic script.

KHITAN, NIU⁄CHIH, AND SI⁄HIA SCRIPTS

Several non⁄Chinese systems of writing are known to have existed in central and north⁄western China in the tenth, eleventh and twelfth centuries A.D. Despite the great impor⁄ tance they once attained, they have long since disappeared as living scripts. The writing of the Khitans, for instance, was for two centuries the official script of the Liao Dynasty of that people: today only five symbols from it are known.

Even more important were the two scripts of the Niu⁄chih, a Tatar people who succeeded the Khitans in the political domination of this part of China. The more ancient of these was adopted in A.D. 1119; the second came into being through revision of the first in 1138.

Finally, there was the ideographic⁄syllabic system of writing of the Tangut or Si⁄Hia (western Hia). From A.D. 982 to 1227, there existed between China and Tibet, on the latter country's northern border, a powerful kingdom called Si⁄Hia (or Hsi⁄Sia). The language spoken by its people, and preserved for us by a Chinese philologist, is the only ancient Tibeto⁄ Burmese language known at present.

Tradition ascribed the invention of this script to king Chao Yüan⁄hao, who was said to have accomplished the task in A.D. 1037. It was a highly refined ideographic⁄syllabic form of writing, and was widely employed for over two centuries. Several inscriptions are extant (the earliest dating from the eleventh century) as well as some manuscripts. The script was written, like Chinese, in columns running from top to bottom, and beginning at the right⁄hand side of the page.

Culturally speaking, at least, Japan has for most of its history been a colony of China. The first cultural contacts between the two countries took place in the last centuries of the first millennium B.C. The traditional view is that these were made through the intermediary of Korea. The details of the earliest stages of the process are uncertain: but it was inevitable, once it had begun, that sooner or later the Chinese system of writing would be introduced into Japan. This event took place at some time in the third or fourth century A.D.

Despite certain ancient traditions to the contrary, the Japanese have never had a truly indigenous writing. The origins of the prehistoric scripts which once existed on the island – the *jindai-moji* or *kamiyo no moji* ('characters of the divine period') – are not completely clear, but it is generally accepted that they were descended from the Nitok script of Korea. There is no connec-tion between these prehistoric scripts and modern Japanese writing.

The adoption of the Chinese script posed many problems for the Japanese. The Chinese language is, as we have seen, essentially monosyllabic and 'isolating' – that is, it does not contain terminations or other grammatical forms. The Japanese language, on the other hand, is polysyllabic and 'agglutinative' – it contains a great many grammatical particles of various kinds.

The problems created by these dissimilarities were further complicated by the fact that the Japanese continued to borrow Chinese characters over a considerable period of time, and from different regions of China. Since Chinese pronunciation has always varied radically from province to province, and since even within a particular area it has undergone profound changes from period to period, the Chinese pronunciation of a particular syllable or word, when the latter was taken over phonetically by the Japanese, never continued for long to be an accurate guide to its pronunciation in Japan.

But phonetic borrowing was not by any means, the only form in which the Chinese script was taken over. At first, indeed, the borrowing was wholly ideogrammatic: the Chinese character for a particular Chinese word was taken over, and then simply pronounced according to its Japanese equivalent; though sometimes it was taken over with its Chinese pronunciation as well (there being, needless to say, no rule or system to guide the acquisition).

Soon it became evident that the differences between the two languages made this simple ideogrammatic transference alone an impracticable one, and some Chinese characters began to be taken over as syllabic (i.e. phonetic) signs, to indicate the various grammatical forms of the Japanese language. Again they were taken over in a quite arbitrary fashion, some entering the script with a Chinese and some with a Japanese pronunciation.

There exists an early example of the new Japanese script which indicates what the resulting confusion was like. The *Kojiki*, a Japanese ancient history composed in A.D. 711–12, was written with Chinese characters *and in a Chinese syntax*: yet, read with the Chinese pronunciation alone it is quite incomprehensible.

Fig. 17

During the eight and ninth centuries A.D., there came into use in Japan a stable syllabic form of writing called *kana* (perhaps from *kanna*, itself a contraction of *kari na*, 'borrowed names'). This took two forms: (1) the *kata kana* or *yamato gana*, used principally in learned works, official documents, and for the transliteration of foreign personal names; and (2) *hira gana*, used for such purposes as grammatical terminations, and also employed for popular literature.

The creation of *kata kana* (='side *kana*', from the fact that it ordinarily appears in addition to Chinese word signs), also

Japanese Syllabaries

Phonetic Value	Katakana	Hiragana	Phonetic Value	Katakana	Hiragana	Phonetic Value	Katakana	Hiragana	Phonetic Value	Katakana	Hiragana
i	イ	い	wa	ワ	わ	w(i)	ヰ	ゐ	sa	サ	さ
ro	ロ	ろ	ka	カ	か	no	ノ	の	ki	キ	き
fa (ha)	ハ	は	yo	ヨ	よ	o	オ	お	yu	ユ	ゆ
ni	ニ	に	ta	タ	た	ku	ク	く	me	メ	め
fo (ho)	ホ	ほ	re	レ	れ	ya	ヤ	や	mi	ミ	み
fe (he)	ヘ	へ	so	ソ	そ	ma	マ	ま	si (shi)	シ	し
to	ト	と	tu (tsu)	ツ	つ	ke	ケ	け	w(e)	ヱ	ゑ
ti (chi)	チ	ち	ne	ネ	ね	fu	フ	ふ	fi (hi)	ヒ	ひ
ri	リ	り	na	ナ	な	ko	コ	こ	mo	モ	も
nu	ヌ	ぬ	ra	ラ	ら	e	エ	え	se	セ	せ
ru	ル	る	mu	ム	む	te	テ	て	su	ス	す
(w)o	ヲ	を	u	ウ	う	a	ア	あ	n	ン	ん

Fig. 17 Japanese syllabaries

called *yamato gana* (='Japanese *kana*'), is traditionally attributed to the minister Kibi, who lived in the eight century A.D. *Hira gana* (='plain' or 'simple *kana*') is attributed to the Buddhist abbot Kobodaishi, who lived at the beginning of the ninth century. Whatever the element of truth in these attributions, it is certain that the period specified for both inventions is correct: both forms were to a large extent adapted from the Chinese characters prevalent, respectively, in the eighth and ninth centuries.

In both forms of *kana* the Chinese symbols were adopted either with their Chinese pronunciation (as it sounded to Japanese ears) or with the contemporary Japanese pronunciation (which differed considerably from that of modern Japanese). Thus, the Chinese ideogram for 'woman', pronounced *mü*, was adopted as the *kana* sign for the word *me*, which means 'woman' in Japanese; while the Chinese sign for 'three', *san*, was adopted for both the Japanese *mi*, 'three', and the Japanese *san*, which also means 'three'.

However, the most important use of the *kana* signs was not for the representation of independent words – these continued, on the whole, to be written in the Chinese characters adopted at an earlier period – but as prepositions, indicators of verb tenses, and phonetic complements. Hence, the *kana* forms cannot be considered full syllabic systems of writing.

Today, the standard script in Japan is *kana-majiri* – that is, Chinese characters with *hira gana* written alongside to give the Japanese pronunciation, and to supply grammatical forms of all kinds. Less frequently used are the forms known as *shin-kata kana* (Chinese characters with *kata kana* alongside; literally a kind of 'side side-kana') and *kunten*, in which Japanese numerals are used with Chinese characters to show the order in which the latter are meant to be read. All these *kana* forms have developed from the *kana* of the eighth and ninth centuries, but, as is apparent, they have never become full syllabic writings of any kind, having never lost their original function as subsidiary forms of assistance to the script proper.

Both *kata kana* and *hira gana*, in their modern guises, contain as a basis the forty-seven syllables of the traditional *kana* scripts, and these constitute the so-called *iroha* (or *irofa*) order of the characters. In addition there is a sign for *n*, which is not pronounced, and two other symbols, bringing the total number of basic *kana* signs to fifty. Altogether these form the *gojū-on* ('fifty sounds') order commonly used in Japanese dictionaries.

The *hira gana* script poses a number of difficulties for those not closely acquainted with it. Its approximately three hundred symbols (with the accretions of the *kana-majiri* form) have many variants, though only one hundred or so are actually used in printed literature. The form itself is so very cursive that frequent ligatures (when it is written by hand) make it extremely difficult for the unadept to read.

Since the Japanese language contains only open syllables – i.e. consonants followed by vowels, and vowels alone – these only are represented in the *kana* scripts. Similar sounds are distinguished by diacritical marks: a *maru* sign (°) distinguishes *p* from *f*; a *nigori* (″) distinguishes *b*, *d*, *g*, *ds* and *z* from *f*, *t*, *k*, *ts*, and *s*, respectively. Since the sound *l* does not exist in Japanese, it is replaced, in the transliteration of European words, by *r* (one of the few aspects of Japanese culture which even the cinema faithfully represents). A tiny sign, *tsu*, indicates the reduplication of a consonant; a thick comma under a syllable plays the same role.

A word should be said about the physical nature of the Japanese scripts. Classical Japanese writing consists of strong bold strokes made in the Chinese fashion, with brush and ink. As in China, years are needed to produce a good calligrapher, and calligraphy is as highly esteemed an art. Originally, the direction of writing was (as in Chinese) in vertical columns running from right to left, though the strokes of the

JAPANESE CALLIGRAPHY
Plate 27

individual characters were made from left to right. Today, no fixed rule is observed. Some books are printed in vertical columns running from left to right, while, in the newer horizontal writing, the lines may run either from left to right or from right to left. The 1942 ruling of the Minister for Instruction, which attempted to enforce a standard direction for the script (horizontal left-to-right), seems to have achieved little in alleviating this confusion.

REFORMS OF JAPANESE WRITING

The total number of characters in the modern Japanese scripts (including all variants) approaches forty thousand, of which only a fraction are in general use. An educated Japanese can read and write approximately two thousand, while a minimum of 1,200 were, until recently, taught in the elementary schools. This is clearly not a system well adapted to the demands of the modern world, and during the past century various attempts have been made to simplify the Japanese scripts in the direction of a true syllabary, an almost inevitable development in a nation which has westernised much of its culture. In 1885, the *Romaji-kai* society was founded. Its aim was the adaptation to the Japanese language of the Latin alphabet, and its magazine, *Romaji-zasshi*, was printed exclusively in Latin characters.

In 1888, the Congress of Orientalists in Paris was presented with a number of texts printed in *kana* characters alone. At about the same time the *Kana no kai* society was founded with the express aim of purifying the *kana* scripts and discouraging the use of ideograms.

In 1900 the Japanese Ministry of Public Education decreed a reduction in the total number of characters to be taught in the schools, and it was at this time that the minimum of 1,200 was established for children on the elementary level. In 1942, as already mentioned, the attempt was made to standardise the direction in which writing was to develop.

With the defeat of Japan in the Second World War, reform

was suggested by the American military government under General MacArthur. An American educational commission called for the abolition from the Japanese scripts of all Chinese derived ideograms, the adaptation to the Japanese language of the Latin alphabet, and the immediate introduction of the new system into popular literature of all kinds.

What the outcome of this modern reforming impulse will be remains, at least for the moment, uncertain. The age seems past when changes of such magnitude in the ingrained cultural habits of a great nation could be enforced overnight by decree. It is one of the more ghastly paradoxes of modern times that it has become a simpler matter to exterminate a civilian population than to change its habits: and writing, in particular, has always exhibited a certain tenaciousness and a resistance to rapid change.

APPENDIX TO CHAPTER III:

EASTER ISLAND SCRIPT

In the Pacific Ocean, 2500 miles west of Chile, lies a spot of and seventy miles across at its widest point. It was discovered on Easter Day 1722 by the Dutch admiral Roggeveen, who gave it the name of Easter Island. It has had other names as well. The Spaniards called it San Carlos, and the indigenous population, of whom there are at present about two hundred, call it – among other things – *Te Pito-te-Henua* ('Navel of the Earth'). It is entirely volcanic, triangular in shape, and curiously symmetrical.

On this island a number of discoveries were made which have fed romantic imaginations for nearly a century. The most immediately striking of these are nearly two hundred colossal stone heads, carved out of a reddish-brown trachytic lava and placed in rows facing the sea. Two of these are now in the

British Museum, and at least one is in New York City. The impression they make is undeniably enigmatic. Some are over thirty feet in height.

Secondly, upon the slopes and headlands of the island im‑ mense walls of large, flat stones were found, likewise facing the sea; and on the landward side of these walls, on a broad terrace, there stand some 250 great stone pedestals marking burial places known to the natives as *abu*. Remains of stone houses measuring nearly one hundred feet by twenty feet were also discovered.

The first record of the third Easter Island 'find' occurred in the late sixties of the last century. At that time Father Roussel of the Catholic Mission on the island (founded 1864) had his attention drawn to a number of wooden tablets covered with a unique form of pictographic writing. How many of these tablets were in existence at that time is uncertain: many seem to have been lost or destroyed. But Father Roussel did send a number of them to Bishop Jaussen of Tahiti; and of these there are today approximately fifteen left.

Fig. 18

The tablets were known to the inhabitants of Easter Island as *kohau‑rongo‑rongo*, though the natives could not read them. They consist chiefly of fragments ranging up to six feet in length. The symbols with which they are covered were incised with sharks' teeth in a kind of *boustrophedon*: the alternate rows are in inverted positions, so that the reader (or rather, the examiner) is obliged to turn the tablet upside down when he reaches the end of each line.

The script is markedly pictographic, though some of the characters are highly stylised. Figures of men, birds, fishes (in‑ cluding such specific varieties as the hammerhead shark) and other animate and inanimate objects can be easily made out.

The tablets have never been deciphered, but traditions cur‑ rent among the inhabitants of the island describe the functions of some of them, or rather the subject matter they deal with:

religious ceremonies, war, prayer, and records of various kinds. It is probable that the characters do not constitute a true script but are memory-aid symbols which had to be supplemented by oral explanation. The contention of Professor I. J. Gelb, that these inscriptions 'are not even writing in the most primitive sense of the word as they probably represent nothing else but pictorial concoctions for magical purposes,' seems excessive. 'Concoction' is rather too strong a word for symbols carefully drawn to a particular scale, neatly grouped in lines, and clearly in a sequence of some sort.

Fig. 18   Inscribed wooden tablet from Easter Island

A far less elaborate form (or a residual remnant?) of the same writing, called by the natives *tau-rongo-rongo*, was still being written on the island sixty or seventy years ago. A specimen of it was obtained from an old and invalid islander towards the end of the last century.

No conclusive evidence has yet appeared to answer any of the problems, historical and linguistic, raised by the discoveries on Easter Island. These problems may be summarised under three headings: (1) By whom were the various monuments on Easter Island built? (2) What connection is there, if any, between the people who constructed the monuments and the island's present inhabitants? (3) Where and by whom was the Easter Island writing created?

There is a tradition among the Easter Islanders of today that the earliest inhabitants came to the island in the twelfth or thirteenth century A.D., bringing with them sixty-seven of the *kohau-rongo-rongo* tablets. There is at least no positive evidence in favour of this tradition: apparently archaeological evidence has been found for an earlier habitation; on the other hand the unconventional number sixty-seven may easily be historically accurate. But even this tradition explains nothing about the origins of the script or of the original inhabitants of the island.

The present population seem to be of Polynesian descent, with a considerable Melanesian element. Their language is a form of the Munda speech, a language once spoken from India eastwards across the Pacific. This lends a superficial credence to the theory of the Hungarian scholar de Hevesy, who has proposed a connection between the Easter Island and the Indus Valley script. This theory must still be classified as completely speculative, since it is supported only by thin external resemblances between the two writings, and is confronted as well by a chronological gap of nearly three millennia. According to the Austrian scholar Robert von Heine-Geldern, the Easter Island script derived from a South-Chinese script used in the period of the Shang-yin dynasty. The original source of this South-Chinese script, of the Chinese script of the Honan bones, and of the Indus Valley script was a Central Asian or Iranian system of writing. All this is highly complicated and problematic.

The German scholar Thomas Barthel, in his *Grundlagen zur Entzifferung der Osterinselschrift* (1958), defines the Easter Island script as a 'conventionalised means of communication, with a limited fund of symbols which can be remarkably increased by means of combinations according to strict rules. But the stage was not one of mere pictography; it was a mixture of ideograms (with one or more meanings). Different levels of symbolisation, and phonetic word-signs were used both to represent names and in *rebus* fashion. Through text-condensation and partial phonetic indication (*Lautandeutung*) understanding is rendered difficult but not impossible.' Whether Barthel's conclusion will receive general acceptance remains to be seen.

CHAPTER IV

Pre-Columbian America

CULTURAL PUZZLE OF PRE-COLUMBIAN AMERICA

THE ANCIENT indigenous cultures of Mexico and Central America present a puzzling challenge to many of our traditional historical categories. The historian is confronted with several peoples who flourished successively, in different degrees, over a length of time corresponding to the period from the late Roman Republic or early Empire to the sixteenth century A.D.; who left behind monumental ruins of various kinds, equal in size and skill of construction to those of many ancient European and Near Eastern civilisations; who employed mathematical and astronomical sciences which remain marvels of exactness, and which were far in advance of those developed by any contemporary European people; and who used a number of very elaborate forms of writing.

So that it is a very short step, for some historians, to speaking of these cultures as 'civilisations', and to comparing their 'level of advancement' with that of the ancient Egyptians, or Babylonians, or Romans. And such speculation seems to have opened the door to something far more clearly undesirable: a wild profusion of theories and speculations, such as have been excited by only a few other subjects, as to the origins of the ancient Mexicans and Central Americans and their possible descent from, ancestry of, or affinities with a multitude of ancient and modern peoples. They have been connected with the Egyptians, Carthaginians, Libyans, Assyrians, Persians, Japanese, Hindus, Eskimos, Tatars, Mongolians, Australasians, Welsh, Irish, and many others. Lord Kingsborough spent a fortune in an effort to prove that they were no less than the descendants of the Ten Lost Tribes of Israel. And one of the most popular theories was, at one time, that they had had their origins on the lost continent of Atlantis.

All this has its ultimate birth in the use of the word 'civilisa-tion' (or some equivalent) to describe the cultures of pre-Columbian America, a usage which is not in fact justified. For in dealing with the Maya, Zapotecs, Toltecs and Aztecs we are not dealing with equivalents of the ancient Near Eastern and European cultures at all. The latter originated and evolved in an interconnected chain of development, in great river valleys situated in a roughly continuous land-area within the northern subtropical belt. They were based, without exception, on the knowledge of writing, the employment of metals, the cultivation of wheat, the domestication of a variety of animals, the use of the wheel, and the growth of large urban centres.

The ancient cultures of Mexico and Central America pre-sent a very different picture. When the Spanish *conquistadores* arrived – the point at which many romanticists envisage flour-ishing civilisations brutally nipped in the bud – no iron tools were used and metallurgy of all kinds was in the most rudi-mentary state, agriculture was severely limited in scale, almost no domestication of animals had been achieved, the weapons employed by the natives were those of savages, and the wheel was unknown for use either in pottery-making or on vehicles. The reader need not be reminded at length that human sacrifice and cannibalism were practised on a considerable scale.

The knowledge that the Great Pyramid of Cholula mea-sures 1,440 feet at the base and is two hundred feet high, or a description of the Mayan calendar, should not be allowed to obscure these overwhelming limitations. What we are con-fronted with in ancient Mexico and Central America are in fact cultures which achieved spectacular advances in one or two fields – notably mathematics, astronomy and chronology – while remaining fundamentally in a state which we shall call 'semi-civilisation': more advanced, certainly, than the North American Indians, but not in any way comparable with the true civilisations of the Egyptians or the peoples of Mesopotamia. All the evidence hitherto found argues, not for some mysterious contact with Europe or the Near East, but for precisely that complete insularity which no evidence has yet appeared to disprove.

What of the writing used in these semi-civilisations? Here we are immensely hampered by the vicious intolerance of the Spanish priests who burned most of the Aztec and nearly all of the Mayan manuscripts. On the basis of what has survived, however, some generalisations are possible. The chief of these is that since both the Mayan and the Aztec writings contain a degree of phonetisation, they must be regarded, in the strict sense, as transitional scripts; but that the phonetisation is of so approximate a kind (e.g. *tepe-tl*, 'mountain', + *yaca-tli*, 'nose,'=Tepeyacac, a place-name; *quauh*, 'forest' or 'tree', + *naua-tl*, 'speech', = *Quauhnawac*, also a place-name), and the narratives so clearly in need of supplementary oral description, that this categorisation is somewhat misleading. As systems, and as regards their basic level of development, the Mayan and Aztec scripts scarcely moved beyond the ideographic stage.

We shall deal with each of the scripts in turn. Although far more is known today about the Aztec than about the Mayan script, the latter will be treated first, in order of chronology.

MAYAN SCRIPT

Until early in the nineteenth century, the semi-civilisation of ancient Mexico was attributed entirely to the Aztecs themselves. Subsequently the Toltecs came to be considered as the transmitters of culture to the former; while now there is general agreement among scholars that the Maya of ancient Central America created the greatest of the pre-Columbian semi-civilisations, and passed on much of their culture to the Toltecs, who were in turn the benefactors of the Aztecs.

The descendants of the Maya still form the bulk of the

population of Yucatan and are found in the neighbouring states of Mexico as well. Today they number about 300,000, and the inclusion of related tribes would bring the total up to approximately 850,000.

The origins of the ancient Mayan culture are at present uncertain. The earliest appearance of this people hitherto revealed by archaeology and exploration was at some time around the first century A.D., in what we now know as the Maya Old Empire. At this time the Mayan culture was already fully developed, especially in its most characteristic aspects: its script, and its astronomical and mathematical knowledge. Such a state of affairs presupposes a long chain of previous development, of which no positive evidence has yet been found. For the alternative possibility, that some form of cultural importation took place, there is at the present time no shred of real proof.

The Maya Old Empire represents the golden age of Mayan art and culture, and saw the rise of the great cities of Palenque (in what is today northern Chiapas) and Copán (western Honduras). In both mathematical and astronomical science the Maya of this period were far ahead of any contemporary people. They had already developed an equivalent for the zero-sign; their calendar, far more accurate than the Julian one which is still in use today, was capable of dealing with a period of five hundred million years.

How and when the Maya invented their script we do not know. But in the earliest examples hitherto found it had already assumed its characteristic form, and shows no structural development or change during the remainder of Mayan history. Only three Mayan manuscripts have been preserved – a state of affairs due largely to the misplaced zeal of Diego de Landa, second Bishop of Yucatan – but we have in addition many beautiful and on the whole well-preserved *stelae*: huge monolithic pillars carved in low relief with glyphs and figures. We

Plate 30

Plate 28

Plate 29
Fig. 19

Fig. 19 Mayan symbols for months UO, ZIP, XUL, YAXKIN, YAX and ZAC, from Codex Dresdensis

have also some large oval stones (altars?), similarly carved; some polychrome clay pottery, with glyphs and figures in paint; and some carvings and engravings on metal, bone and wood.

On the whole, with the exception of the calendrical symbols and some notation signs, the Mayan script remains undeciphered: and this is made all the sadder by the fact that first-hand knowledge of the script and its meaning disappeared only two and a half centuries ago. According to Spanish sources, records in Mayan script continued to be made until the end of the seventeenth century: and although this late script may not have been identical with that of the pre-Columbian period, there is no doubt that a knowledge of it would help greatly in the work of decipherment and interpretation.

As matters stand we can say with certainty only that the Mayan script which first appears under the Old Empire was a pictorial, though already quite conventionalised, form of writing, partly ideographic, and probably partly phonetic as well.

For such information as we possess beyond this bare minimum we are dependent, paradoxically enough, on that same Diego de Landa who was responsible for the wholesale destruction of Mayan manuscripts. He has proved a far from completely trustworthy source in this respect, since his account and transcription of the Mayan 'alphabet' has failed completely to elucidate the Mayan documents we possess. It is not known whether this was a deliberate fabrication on his part, an ingenious trick played by Mayan informants, or simply a misunderstanding by de Landa of the actual nature of the script. Perhaps it was some combination of these factors.

Thanks to Landa's *Relacion de las cosas de Yucatan* (1556) – or rather, to that part of the work which has survived – we can at least read the Mayan symbols for days and months.

The Mayan calendar was an extraordinarily complex affair. The day was called *kin*, 'the sun'. The next unit was the month, of which there were two kinds: *u*, 'moon', consisting of thirty days; and *unial* (twenty days) which was the basis of *tun*, the solar year. The latter consisted of eighteen *uinals* plus five supplementary days called *xma kaba kin*, 'days without name', or, alternatively, *u yail kin*, 'the unfortunate days' – they were considered a most unlucky time of year: in short, taboo. There was no leap year, but the length of the ordinary tropical year was, as we shall see, determined with extreme accuracy.

Twenty *tun* formed a *katun* or *edad* of 7,200 days; and twenty *katun* made up in turn a *bactun* of 144,000 days. The days were numbered from 1 to 13. An arbitrary period of 260 days, called *tzolkin*, coordinated with the *tun-katun-bactun* cycle, resulted in the Mayan grand cycle of approximately (in terms of our own calendar) 256 years, the entire system being, as we have said, phenomenally accurate.

The Mayan system of numeration was vigesimal (i.e. based on the number 20). The character for zero (already present in their system) was shaped like a shell; the numerals 1, 2, 3 and 4 were represented by dots; 5, 10 and 15 by sticks, lines or bars. The numeral 20 may have been represented by the moon, though this is not certain: while the symbols for multiples of 20 (*e.g.* 400, 8,000, 160,000) are also not definitely known, though they may have been indicated by the 'place-value' system.

That writing was considered by the Maya themselves to be of great importance may be seen from their attribution of its invention to their most important deity, Itzamna, son of the Creator-god Hunab-Ku. This is confirmed by the report of Landa and other contemporary Spanish writers that a knowledge of the script was limited to the priests, their sons, and some of the principal lords: and that not even all the priests knew how to read it. We have already seen a similar phenomenon in our examination of Egyptian hieroglyphic writing: the sacredness or awesomeness of a script being most effectually maintained when its use is closely restricted. This accounts too, perhaps, for the fact that the Mayan script changed so little in its fundamentals during the entire span of its recorded existence.

TOLTECS About the middle of the first millennium A.D., a people who called themselves the *Aculhuaque* ('strong' or 'tall' men) entered Mexico, and, some time around the year A.D. 770, arrived at the site of their future capital, Tollan. Their origins are uncertain, but they were the first immigrants into the Valley of Mexico to speak a dialect belonging to the Nahuan group of languages. Their culture, borrowed to a good extent from the Maya, reached its apogee around the end of the ninth century; and the pyramids, temples, palaces and storeyed houses they built earned them the name of *Toltecs* ('skilled workers') from their eventual successors, the Aztecs. Little is known, however, about their writing, as only a few Toltec glyphs have come down to us.

CHICHIMECA AND OTOMI At the end of the tenth century A.D. the country of the Toltecs was invaded by the less civilised Chichimeca, who also spoke a Nahuan dialect, and the Toltecs disappeared from the historical horizon. The Chichimecan supremacy was brief: a period of warfare followed between themselves and various other tribes, and for a time the Otomi (a non-Nahuan people) held sway. Then, at some time in the twelfth century A.D., the Aztecs settled in the country.

AZTEC SCRIPT

According to their own tradition, the Aztecs began their migration (perhaps in A.D. 1168) from the island of Aztlan (='Aztec place') somewhere in the north. That they did come from the north is certain, though the island must still be regarded as mythical. In A.D. 1325, for reasons of defence, they settled on the salt marshes at the western edge of Lake Tezcuco (or Texcoco). Their original settlement there probably comprised a number of pile-dwellings standing in the water.

From it grew the town of Tenochtitlán, ancestor of the modern Mexico City.

A century passed after their settlement at Tenochtitlán before they succeeded in establishing themselves as one of the most important peoples of the Anahuac, the Mexican plateau. Around 1430, under their ruler Itzcoatl, they formed a league with two neighbouring states, becoming thereby the leading member of an Aztec confederacy. Now, under a series of warrior-rulers, they embarked on a period of expansion and conquest which only the arrival of the Spaniards halted: their chief purposes being, not political domination, but loot, tribute, and great numbers of prisoners for their human sacrifices. Some Mexican tribes remained independent, however, and continued to wage war against the Aztecs until the arrival of the *conquistadores*. The Spanish victory over the natives was greatly facilitated by these savage feuds and hatreds.

The semi-civilisation of the Aztecs was a mosaic of elements borrowed from other cultures, chiefly the Maya and the Toltec. They achieved an impressive skill in metal-working and architecture, but even in these respects they do not seem to have shown any considerable originality. Their mathematical and astronomical knowledge was probably of Mayan origin.

Although a straightforward adoption by the Aztecs (or the Toltecs) of the Mayan script did not take place, there being no likeness in the external form of the two scripts, there is little doubt that the Mexican peoples received at least the *idea* of writing from the Maya. Although this makes the Aztec script an offshoot of the Mayan, there is general agreement today that the former is degenerative in character, moving not in the direction of simplicity or utility but of over-eleboration, and having nothing of the aesthetic beauty of some of the Mayan inscriptions.

We must be thankful that a fair number of Aztec manuscripts survived the zeal of the Spanish priests, and that in

Plate 31

consequence we know a fair amount about the script. Even more than that of the Maya, it was a highly pictorial form of writing: almost all its symbols were pictures of one kind or another. It was technically a transitional script, many of its conventional signs having a phonetic value. These phonograms were either word-signs or syllables, and they were used principally in the writing of personal and place-names, and the names of deities (a procedure also facilitated by the *ikonomatic* system, used for the representation of personal men's names like 'Smoking Star' and 'Jaguar Claw').

Nevertheless, the phonetisation was often, as in the Mayan system, of a very approximate kind, giving only the rough pronunciation of the word in question. The efforts of the scribes seem to have been directed almost completely in an ideographic direction, towards the idea rather than the sound, whenever sustained narrative of any sort was called for. Hence, the script is almost always in need of supplementary oral description, and can with more justice be called ideographic than transitional.

The greater part of the so-called Aztec 'codices' which have come down to us are devoted to divination, ritual and astrology. A few are concerned primarily with genealogies and political events, making up a kind of rough chronicle or history. Those done before the arrival of the Spaniards were chiefly written by the native priests, whose duties included the keeping of religious, legal and political records. Such manuscripts as were written after the Spanish conquest deal principally with historical and religious (Catholic) matters: a well-known example being the Aztec catechism written at some time in the sixteenth century.

The 'codices' were made of either coarse cloth or a kind of paper called *amatl*, folded in screen-fashion to form 'pages'. Before folding, the sheet was approximately six or seven inches wide: it was cut to varying lengths, depending upon the desired length of the 'codex'. The surface was covered with a very thin coating of white varnish to receive the text, the latter being painted on both sides in a wide range of colours which included red, yellow, blue, green, purple, brown, and orange. The colours were outlined in black.

The folding sheet was fastened at one end to what might be called the 'binding' of the manuscript: a thin, rectangular sheet of wood, brilliantly varnished, of nearly the same size as the leaves. The 'binding' had no back.

The Aztec 'codices' have been partially deciphered. Many of the deities mentioned in them have been identified, the personal and place-names can be read, and some of the ceremonies they record can now be understood. Yet much remains to be done, and much of the decipherment which has been achieved hitherto is only tentative. Even the classification of the manuscripts by area and tribe (Aztec proper, Zapotec, Xicalanca, Mixtec, etc.) is not always certain or possible. Extensive work is now being done in this field, however, and there is no doubt that progress is being made towards full decipherment. *

DECIPHER-
MENT OF
AZTEC
SCRIPT

* A note on recent decipherment of Mayan Script will be found on p. 178

CHAPTER V
Phonetic scripts and the Alphabet

As WE HAVE ALREADY SEEN, the prototypal development of a script is ordinarily from embryo-writing through
pictography to the ideographic stage. If there is any further
development after this point (aside from purely external changes
in the form of the script), then this is invariably in a phonetic
direction of some kind.

These last three words, 'of some kind', sum up the crux of the
problem: for with the transition to a phonetic (or semi-phonetic) form of writing, many complications crowd on to the
scene: polyphones, homophones, and other forms requiring
phonetic complements and determinatives of various kinds.
These complications put grave difficulties in the way of a
script becoming, not progressively more unwieldy, but a truly
flexible instrument of communication. We have seen, for instance, how Egyptian hieroglyphic writing became increasingly cluttered with determinatives, and how, with the introduction of *hsing shêng*, the total number of symbols in the Chinese
script grew to excess.

We may, metaphorically, liken these complications to a
forest in which a personified Script wanders, increasingly
hampered by thorns, briars and unexpected pitfalls. Succour
lies at the other end of this wood, in the form of the realisation
that the basic building-block of all speech and all languages is
the syllable; that the number of different syllables in a language
is in most cases comparatively restricted; and that salvation lies
in the adoption of a systematically syllabic form of writing.
It becomes evident how thorny a place our forest is when we
consider that of all the scripts we have hitherto examined none
achieved a successful 'break-through', though a few moved
haltingly towards it. It is significant, too, that it should have
been the Persians, in an apparently deliberate and conscious

adaptation of neo-Babylonian cuneiform to an Indo-European tongue, who succeeded in creating a true phonetic system (indeed, something very close to an alphabet); though they did this several centuries after the Semitic alphabet had been taken over by the Greeks, and at a time when the Aramaic alphabet had already achieved a wide currency throughout the Near East. The Japanese, attempting a comparable transformation of a script already rooted and established, have hitherto been un successful.

It is evident that the achievement of an at least *semi*-phonetic writing is one of the most important stages in the simplification of a script, and that, historically, the appearance of such semi-phonetic scripts in the Near East preceded (and was probably a necessary preliminary to) the invention of that most wieldy of script-forms, the Alphabet. Hence, the examination of three 'pure' syllabaries cannot fail to be of interest, even though it is certain that two of them appeared well after the invention of alphabetic writing.

PSEUDO-HIEROGLYPHIC SCRIPT OF BYBLOS

Aldous Huxley's essay, *Adonis and the Alphabet*, has perhaps made the ancient Phoenician town of Byblos familiar to most readers. Its associations with the history of writing could not be more intimate or important. In addition to being a virtual quarry for various ancient writings, its name provided the Greeks with a word for 'book', and so was the ultimate ancestor of our own name for Holy Scripture.

In 1929, the French archaeologist Maurice Dunand discovered at Byblos the first of a number of texts in a script unknown until then. Subsequently, nine additional inscriptions were excavated, the total find comprising two bronze tablets, four bronze *spatulae*, one stone *stele*, and three stone fragments (two of which may be pieces of one and the same inscription,

Fig. 20 Stone fragment, inscribed in pseudo-hieroglyphic script, from Byblos

in which case the total quantity would be brought down to nine).

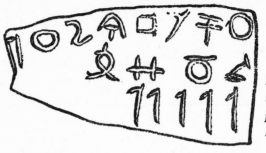

Fig. 21 *Bronze spatula, inscribed in pseudo-hieroglyphic script, from Byblos*

M. Dunand published the results of his studies in 1945, indicating that the scripts contained a total of 114 different signs (the leading orientalist W. F. Albright increases this to between 125 and 150). He grouped them into a number of classes on the basis of their pictorial representations: animals (thirteen signs), vegetation (thirteen), tools (as many as twenty-six), cult-symbols (six), navigation (ten), geometric (eight), undetermined objects (seventeen), and twelve signs which are either completely uncertain, or damaged in the texts. Of these 114 symbols, approximately fifty are, according to M. Dunand, similar to certain characters of the Egyptian hieroglyphic writing.

Dunand expressed the opinion that the 114 signs which had been identified did not constitute all the symbols in the script; and that the script was either a transitional form of writing (with a possible use of determinatives) or a syllabic system. He argued that this 'pseudo-hieroglyphic' script had originated around the twenty-second century B.C. under Egyptian influence, and that it probably represented an important further development and simplification of the Egyptian consonantal system.

Finally, M. Dunand put forward the assertion that although the few extant documents in the pseudo-hieroglyphic writing do not allow us to formulate a chronology of the script's development, the discovery of the so-called Asdrubal *spatula*, containing a Phoenician alphabetic inscription and some scratchings in a form of the pseudo-hieroglyphic script, indicated that the latter was still in use at a time when the Alphabet had been invented (the *spatula* being dated, by himself, to the fourteenth century B.C.): and from here he went on to argue that the pseudo-hieroglyphic script of Byblos was the prototype of the Alphabet.

Other scholars have disagreed considerably, however, with M. Dunand's dating. The most recent estimates place all the pseudo-hieroglyphic inscriptions between the eighteenth and fifteenth centuries B.C. If this estimate is the correct one, then whatever influence may have passed between the Byblian pseudo-hieroglyphic script and the Alphabet would have moved in quite the contrary direction: from the extant Semitic alphabet to the pseudo-hieroglyphic writing.

More recently, Professor Edouard Dhorme, the well-known French Orientalist, put forward a decipherment of the Byblos inscriptions. The pseudo-hieroglyphic writing, he maintains, is definitely a syllabic script representing the Phoenician language, there being no connection between the objects pictorially represented by the signs and their phonetic values. According to Professor Dhorme, over one hundred symbols were borrowed by the Phoenicians from foreign scripts, particularly the Egyptian hieroglyphic writing; and the Byblos texts are to be dated, not in the twenty-second century B.C. (after Dunand), but in the period of the Pharaoh Amenophis IV: that is, at approximately 1375 B.C. Professor Dhorme's estimate is that the pseudo-hieroglyphic script contains a total of approximately one hundred signs.

Professor Dhorme published a number of translated texts from the Byblos inscriptions, together with a syllabic table of the script. There are some ambiguities in his explanations, however, and until these are clarified, or until further significant studies or discoveries are made, the precise nature, origin and dating of the Byblos inscriptions must be held tentatively *sub judice*.

CYPRIOTE SYLLABARY

In the ancient world the island of Cyprus, forty-four miles from the eastern coast of the Mediterranean and a few days' sail from Egypt and Crete, was a great metallurgical centre and a coveted strategic outpost. Like other areas which provided meeting-grounds for a variety of cultural influences, ancient Cyprus seems to have been the scene of considerable experiment in writing.

The earliest example of writing so far found on the island is a linear inscription on the handle of a pitcher, attributed to Period III of the Early Bronze Age: *c.* 2400–2100 B.C. The nature of this script is uncertain: there are some resemblances to Minoan pictographic writing, but these are too tenuous for any definite conclusions to be drawn. It is possible that this was an indigenous script of the native Cypriotes before the Mycenaean Greeks established themselves on the island in the fifteenth century B.C.

A span of well over half a millennium separates the inscription on this jar from the second-oldest documents found: inscriptions in the so-called Cypro-Mycenaean writing which was used on the island from about 1400 B.C. until the middle of the eleventh century B.C.: a span corresponding almost exactly with the period of Mycenaean occupation. It is nearly certain, therefore, that the Cypro-Mycenaean script was either brought by the Mycenaeans themselves, or, what is more probable, originated under their rule and influence. It is at least *possible*, therefore, that the Cypro-Mycenaean writing is an adaptation of Mycenaean Linear B to the representation of the

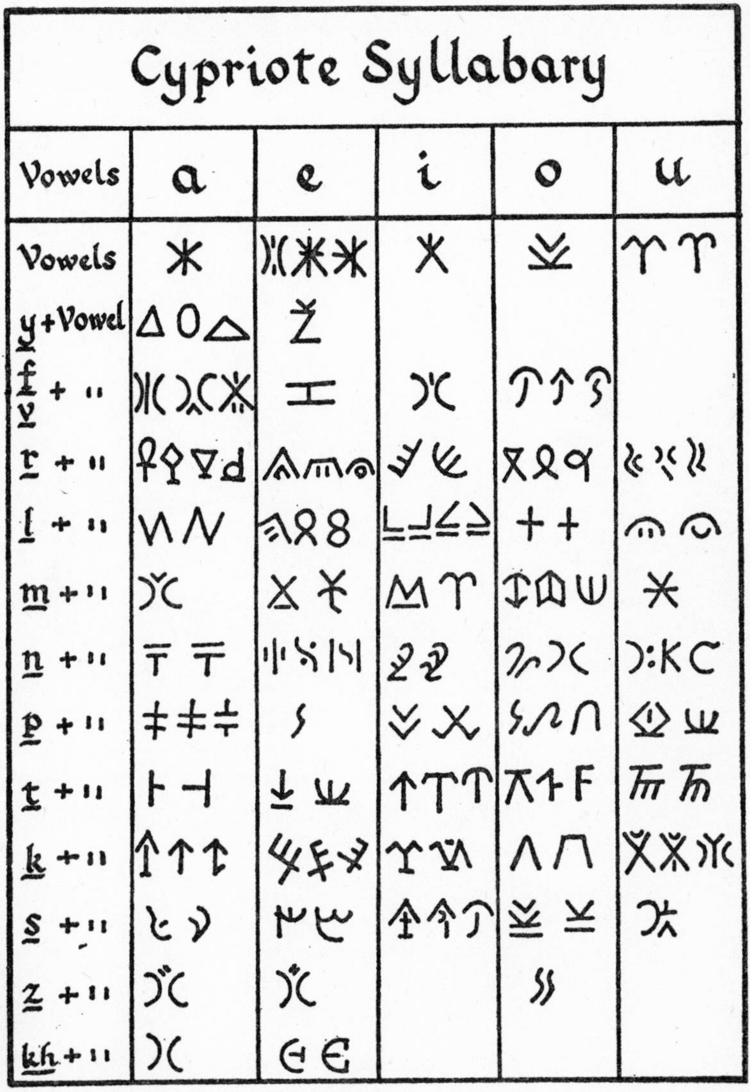

Fig. 22 *Cypriote Syllabary*

indigenous Cypriote language (whatever that may have been); but it is still too early to tell whether this was the case, or whether Ventris's decipherment may have some bearing on the subject.

Between the Cypro-Mycenaean script and the earliest known examples of the Cypriote syllabary proper, there is once again a considerable gap. Cypro-Mycenaean continued to be used, as we have mentioned, until the middle of the eleventh century B.C.; the Cypriote syllabary was in use, so far as we know, from about 700 B.C. down to the first century B.C.

The majority of the Cypriote syllabic inscriptions hitherto found, approximately 185 in number, are couched in Greek, a few in an undeciphered (? indigenous) language. Most of these inscriptions date from the fifth and fourth centuries B.C. There is a paucity of inscriptions from the earliest period of its use.

Fig. 22

The Cypriote syllabary is a linear script consisting of approximately forty-five symbols. These are made up of combinations of strokes, straight, semicircular and circular, which give the entire syllabary a somewhat geometric appearance. Each sign represents an open syllable (e.g. *pa, ko, ne, se, ru, ki*) or a vowel. The script was clearly developed for setting down a non-Greek tongue, perhaps the indigenous language in which a few of the inscriptions seem to be couched, and its representation of Greek sounds is therefore highly imperfect. Thus, *Aphrodite* was written in the Cypriote syllabary as *a-po-ro-ti-ta-i; basileous* as *pa-si-le-ve-o-se*, ptolin as *po-to-li-ne*, and so forth. The writing was generally arranged from right to left, though sometimes from left to right or in *boustrophedon*. The decipherment of the syllabary is still incomplete. The possibly Anatolian affinities of the Bronze Age Cypriotes may give some clue as to the indigenous language of the Cypriote syllabary. Anthropological deductions indicate that this population was of Armenoid stock, which also included the Hittites and other west Asiatic peoples.

PERSIAN CUNEIFORM

We have had occasion to mention this remarkable script before. A conscious adaptation of neo-Babylonian cuneiform, it became the official script of the Persian Achaemenid dynasty under whose rule, from 550 B.C. to the conquests of Alexander the Great in the fourth century B.C., the Persians were indeed the most powerful people of western Asia. Persian cuneiform probably originated in the reign of either Cyrus the Great (550–529 B.C.) or Darius the Great (521–486 B.C.), and resulted in the establishment of a syllabic – indeed, quasi-alphabetic – script, which had no more than its external form in common with the earlier cuneiform writings of Mesopotamia.

Persian cuneiform consisted of forty-one symbols, of which four were ideograms ('king,' 'province,' 'country,' and 'Awra-Mazda') and one a sign for the division between words. The remainder were phonetic symbols, which may be divided into five groups:

(1) three vowels (*a, i, u*). The Persian long *a* was represented by the ordinary *a* repeated twice.

(2) thirteen consonants (*kh, ch, th, p, b, f, y, l, s, z, sh, thr, h*) each of which could have the value of a pure consonant, or of a consonant followed by the short *a*.

(3) ten symbols for the consonants *q* (hard *k*), *g, t, n, r*. Each of these consonants could be represented in two different ways. The first of these indicated that it was to be read as a pure consonant (e.g. simply as *q* or *g*), or, alternatively, as the same consonant followed by a short *a* (e.g. *qa, ga*). The second form indicated that it was to be read with the addition of the vowel (e.g. *qu, gu*).

(4) two alternative forms for writing the consonants *dj* and *w* (four symbols altogether):
(a) as pure consonants, or followed by short *a*.
(b) as the same consonants, followed by *i*.

(5) six symbols for the consonants *d* and *m*, representing three alternative forms in which each could be written:
(a) as pure consonants, or followed by short *a*.
(b) as the same consonants, followed by *u*.
(c) as the same consonants, followed by *i*.

Persian cuneiform was written from left to right. As we have already indicated, its quasi-alphabetic quality probably reveals the influence of the already widespread Aramaic alphabet.

ORIGIN OF THE ALPHABET

The history of the Alphabet from the end of the second millennium B.C. to the present time is, on the whole, clear, though many details, and the interrelations of some particular alphabetic scripts, are still uncertain. It is the prehistory and the protohistory of the Alphabet which remain wrapped in comparative obscurity, a fog which is only gradually lifting: so that anyone interested in the subject must examine reams of interpretation and counter-interpretation, ranging from the highly well informed to the simply speculative, and continuing downward to the utterly irresponsible.

The origin of the Alphabet has been a matter for study and speculation since ancient times. In the *Annals* of Tacitus, for instance, we read that:

The first people to represent thoughts graphically were the Egyptians with their animal-pictures. These earliest records of humanity are still to be seen, engraved on stone. They also claim to have discovered the letter and taught them to the Phoenicians, who, controlling the seas, intro duced them to Greece and were credited with inventing what they had really borrowed. (xi–14: transl. based on Grant).

That little was added to this store of knowledge in the next seventeen hundred years (indeed, that something was lost) can be seen from Gibbon's footnote to his statement that 'Phoenicia and Palestine will for ever live in the memory of mankind; since America, as well as Europe, has received letters from the one, and religion from the other':

The use of letters was introduced among the savages of Europe about fifteen hundred years before Christ; and the Europeans carried them to America, about fifteen centuries after the Christian æra. But in a period of three thousand years, the Phoenician alphabet received considerable alterations, as it passed through the hands of the Greeks and Romans. (*Decline and Fall*, ed. Bury, I: i, *n*. 90).

Not until the nineteenth century was a new vein of study opened up in regard to the Alphabet, and then it followed naturally upon the great discoveries in Egypt, Mesopotamia and Palestine. That Phoenicia was the starting point for all speculation on the subject had been known long before Tacitus. The question now was, from whom had the Phoenicians obtained this inimitable invention? Or, if its use was indigenous to Phoenicia, how and when did it originate?

To trace the history of scholarly thought and dispute on this subject since the last three decades of the nineteenth century would be a pointless affair. Suffice it to say that the 'sources' suggested for the Alphabet were, in turn, Egypt, Sumer, Babylonia, Assyria, Cyprus (the Cypriote syllabary), Asia Minor (Hittite hieroglyphics), and Crete. Insofar as they assumed a direct derivation, all these theories have had to be discarded.

Today, a discussion of the origins of the Alphabet must

take into close consideration the remarkable, sometimes re-volutionising archaeological discoveries of the past three de-cades in Palestine, Syria and Sinai. Indeed, these discoveries, though they have not, needless to say, been made according to a plan of any kind – archaeology will never be so streamlined a discipline – have progressively clarified a subject in which the true scholar and the crank could once wage war on a nearly equal footing. Each new discovery has shed light on those which preceded it; and so a discussion of the subject today must differ considerably from one on the same subject of fifty or even thirty years ago.

EARLIEST
NORTH-
SEMITIC
INSCRIP-
TIONS

The most convenient point of departure for our discussion is the North-Semitic alphabet (henceforth occasionally abbre-viated to *N.S.A.*), which was, until quite recently, the earliest alphabetic writing that could with certainty be identified as such.

In the first quarter of this century, knowledge of the native epigraphy of Syria and Palestine was limited and uncertain. The discovery of the Mesh' Stone (cf. 2 *Kings* iii, 4–27) in 1868 had confirmed the existence of a Semitic alphabetic script in the middle of the ninth century B.C., but none of the other Semitic inscriptions subsequently found antedated this period.

Plate 36

Then, in 1923, the French scholar P. Montet found at Byblos the Akhiram Sarcophagus, inscribed with an epitaph in what has since been designated as the North-Semitic alphabetic writing. Although there has been some scholarly disagreement over the dating of the Akhiram epitaph, it now seems reasonably certain that it can be placed in the eleventh century B.C. Other North-Semitic inscriptions have been discovered, which belong to a slightly earlier or later

Plate 38
Plate 46

period. These included the Yekhimilk inscription (eleventh century), the Gezer Calendar (c. 1000 B.C.), the Roueisseh spearhead inscription (c. eleventh-tenth century), and the Abiba'al and Eliba'al inscriptions (tenth century).

From these discoveries there gradually emerged the picture
f a prototypal form of alphabetic writing, the above-mentioned
North-Semitic, consisting of twenty-two symbols written
niformly from right to left: a consonantal writing which is
ow regarded as the direct ancestor of the Hebrew, Moabite,
Phoenician, Aramaic, and Greek scripts, and which was de-
nitely in existence in the last centuries of the second millenium B.C.

In 1929 the discovery was made at Ugarit (modern Râs   UGARITIC
Shamrah, on the Syrian coast) of the first of hundreds of clay   CUNEIFORM
ablets inscribed in a *cuneiform* alphabet of thirty-two letters,   ALPHABET
nknown until then. This was an epoch-making find, for it
pened to Semitic scholars an entire Canaanite literature of
mmense value, casting light on (among other things) many
arts of the Old Testament. The Ugaritic script has no con-   *Figs 23, 24*
ection with the various cuneiform scripts of Mesopotamia

'a	9	w	17	m	25	s̩²(ṭ,z̧ ?)	
'i-'e	10	z	18	n	26	q	
'u-'o	11	ḥ	19	s'	27	r	
b	12	ḫ	20	sᶻ	28	sh'	
g	13	ṭ	21	˙	29	sh²(s'?)	
d	14	y	22	ġ	30	s̀(?)th(?) ṯ(?)	
ḏ	15	k	23	p	31	ž	
h	16	l	24	ṣ'	32	t	

Fig. 23   Cuneiform alphabet of Ugarit (Râs Shamrah)

except insofar as it was, like the latter, impressed with a stylus in wet clay. Mesopotamian influence may also be indicated by the fact that the extant Ugaritic inscriptions were written from left to right, unlike the North-Semitic alphabetic writings: the only exceptions to this rule being, interestingly enough, three *Palestinian* inscriptions written in a version of Ugaritic cuneiform, all three of which run from right to left. A few of the tablets date from the fifteenth century B.C.; the bulk from the fourteenth.

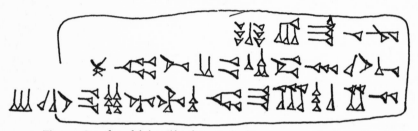

Fig. 24   Cuneiform alphabet-tablet of Ugarit: the oldest extant example of a complete ABC

The cuneiform alphabet of Ugarit bears all the marks of deliberate invention, and it is now safe to say that its inventor or inventors were almost certainly influenced by an already extant Semitic alphabet which was earlier in time than, and was probably the direct ancestor of, the North-Semitic alphabet. It was perhaps also influenced by the pseudo-hieroglyphic script of Byblos, and certainly by some of the other scripts current in the same period. It is possible that it answered the needs of natives of Ugarit who knew of the Alphabet's existence and recognised its extreme usefulness, but who were accustomed to the use of clay and stylus. Six of the letters in Ugaritic cuneiform directly resemble Semitic alphabetic letters having the same phonetic values.

In itself, the cuneiform alphabet of Ugarit testifies to the probable existence of a Semitic alphabetic script in at least the sixteenth or fifteenth century B.C.

In 1904-5, Sir William Flinders Petrie discovered in Sinai a number of inscriptions which, although they bore some external resemblances to Egyptian hieroglyphic writing, contained so few different characters as to suggest the possibility of their being a form of alphabetic writing. Subsequent discoveries raised the total of extant Palaeo-Sinaitic inscriptions to approximately twenty-five.

In 1916, the egyptologist Dr A. H. (now Sir Alan) Gardiner announced a partial decipherment of these texts. He argued from the acrophonic principle: to wit, that the characters of the Palaeo-Sinaitic writing, if they were alphabetic, derived their phonetic values from the pronunciation of the initial consonants of the ideograms from which they were descended. His solution was based on an extremely ingenious method of reading a single 'clump' of characters which seemed to recur in several of the texts in question, and pronouncing these characters according to the initial consonants of their Semitic cognates. These single symbols were, respectively, a shepherd's crook (Heb. *lamed*), a house (Heb. *bêth*), an eye (Heb. *'ayin*), a second shepherd's crook (*lamed*), and a cross (Heb. *taw*); the result was an initial reading of *l-b-'-l-t*. Gardiner argued that this should be read (with inserted vowels) as *le-Ba'alat*, 'to the Lady Ba'alath': an argument which derived additional weight from the fact that Ba'alath was the main Semitic female deity, and equivalent to the Egyptian Hathor.

For many years Gardiner's theory could not be generally accepted, despite its ingenuity. The research and labour of many students made no further progress in the decipherment of the Sinaitic inscriptions; and Gardiner himself had written: 'Unfortunately... I have no suggestions for the reading of any other word, so that the decipherment of the name Ba'alat must remain, so far as I am concerned, an unverifiable hypothesis.'

In 1948, an expedition of the University of California under W. F. Albright achieved more positive results in the deci-

Fig. 25 Early Canaanite inscriptions (see also Plates 32-34); they may be divided into three groups:
I, attributed to the eighteenth or seventeenth century B.C.: 1, Gezer potsherd; 2, Shechem stone plaque,
3, Lachish dagger; II, fourteenth century B.C.: 4, Tell el Hesy inscription; 5, Tell el 'Ajjūl pot; 6, Beth-
Shemesh ostracon; III, thirteenth century B.C.: 7, 8 (see also next Figure), 10 and 11, inscriptions found in
Lachish. This group also includes 9, an engraved stone of a later date which clearly resembles some of the
Lachish signs from the foundations of the Temple of Jerusalem

pherment of the Sinaitic inscriptions. In Albright's opinion, it was established with certainty: (1) that they were alphabetic in nature, (2) that they were written in a Canaanite dialect, and (3) that Gardiner's partial decipherment had been quite correct. The inscriptions date from approximately the beginning of the sixteenth century B.C.

EARLY
CANAANITE
INSCRIP-
TIONS
Fig. 25

In the past three decades, the probable origin of the alphabet has been pushed back even further by the discovery, in 1929, 1934 and 1937, of three inscriptions generally attributed to the eighteenth or seventeenth century. These are: (1) the Gezer potsherd, (2) the Shechem stone plaque, and (3) the Lachish

dagger. Although the last-named was found in the same year
as the Shechem plaque, 1934, the inscription on it was only
discovered three years later, when it was cleaned. The writing
of these inscriptions has been named (for convenience) the
Early Canaanite script.

Altogether, these three inscriptions contain a total of only
fourteen letters (ten separate characters). For the present, at
least, this seems to rule out the possibility of complete decipherment. Nevertheless, it is certain that three of the characters –
cognates of the Hebrew *yod, resh* and *beth* – are identical with the
corresponding characters in the Sinaitic inscriptions, and that,
like the latter, the Early Canaanite script was ordinarily written
in a vertical direction. There is at least a strong possibility
that these three inscriptions represent the earliest alphabetic
writing yet discovered.

It must be remembered, however, that our position in regard
to the history of the Alphabet in the period 1800–1200 B.C.
is rather like that of travellers flying high over a mountain range
on a cloudy day. Here and there a peak or a plateau juts out of
the mists, and it is comparatively easy to determine their relative
heights; yet, to picture in the imagination the topography of the
entire range – the precise geological relationship of peak to
peak – is impossible. It is just as idle and premature to speculate
in a facile fashion on the Early Canaanite alphabet, seeing in
it a 'forerunner' of the Palaeo-Sinaitic alphabet, and in the
latter the 'ancestor' of the North-Semitic alphabet. That they

Plate 32

Plates 33, 34
Fig. 26

*Fig. 26 Early
Canaanite in-
scription from
Lachish. Thir-
teenth century
B.C. (see also
Fig. 25, 8 and
Plate 34)*

119

are closely related is certain; what the exact relationships were, and what other alphabetic writings may have existed within the same period, is for time and archaeology to discover.

We *can* say with certainty, though, that the turbulent Hyksos period in Syria, Palestine and Egypt (*c.* 1730–1580 B.C.), with its uprooting established cultural and ethnic patterns in the Fertile Crescent, favoured creative experimentation in writing and therefore provided a likely time for the break-through to the conception of an alphabetic script. This break-through had probably been accomplished by the time of the Gezer, Shechem and Lachish inscriptions.

LIKELY
PLACE OF
ORIGIN OF
THE
ALPHABET

Of all the areas in the Near East, the region of Palestine and Syria provides the most likely source for the invention of the Alphabet. It formed, as has frequently been pointed out, a kind of bridge uniting the great civilisations of Egypt and Meso-potamia. Large Egyptian trading posts were established in this region, cuneiform tablets have been found at various sites throughout it, and influences from Crete and Cyprus made themselves felt, as did the culture of the Hittites. In itself this may sound like air rushing into a vacuum; but the Syrian littoral is now known to have had a highly developed culture in the second millennium B.C., which received, transformed and re-transmitted these influences. And in the Hyksos period, which almost certainly encompasses the creation of the Alphabet, Palestine and Syria were jointly (if an irreverent parallel be admitted) the Victoria Station of the eastern Mediterranean.

That the second-earliest alphabetic writing known today should have been found in Sinai, and that its earliest analysts, Gardiner and Sethe, thought it an intermediate form between the Egyptian hieroglyphic writing and the North-Semitic alphabet, should by no means cast doubt on this tentative location of the Alphabet's place of origin. The inventor or inventors of the Alphabet were certainly influenced by Egyp-

ian hieroglyphic writing: the really surprising thing would be
f no such influence were discernible. Since the Alphabet was
an invention requiring great intelligence (indeed, genius), there
is little doubt that the man or men who invented it were acquainted with, or aware of, most of the scripts current in the
eastern Mediterranean at the time. The reader need scarcely be
reminded that a knowledge of Egyptian hieroglyphic writing
was not confined to Egypt itself, or even to its immediate
environs.

Nor should we exclude the possibility that a single man was
in fact responsible for the conceptual leap involved in the
creation of this unique form of writing: the leap from what had
previously been achieved – imperfectly phonetic writings of
various kinds – to the idea of representing each single sound by
a single unvarying symbol. It is the kind of sudden intuitive
perception which single men like Newton have more than
once accomplished, even when others did the elaborating and
the perfecting.

Thus much do we know, and thus much can we, perhaps
with safety, speculate. But a single example will serve to illus-
trate how profound the gaps in our knowledge are. The reader
will perhaps have wondered at the use of the phrase 'North-
Semitic alphabet': why not simply *Semitic* alphabet, since its
use seems to have extended over a good part of Syria and most
of Palestine? The answer is that the phrase is used to distinguish
the N.S.A. from the South-Semitic alphabet which, although
it remained within the confines of the Arabian Peninsula for
most of its history, may have been as old as the North-Semitic
alphabet in its origins, and was probably neither derived from,
nor directly dependent upon, the latter. It was definitely in use
at the beginning of the first millennium B.C. The most that
can be said (or rather, speculated) about its origins is that it
may have been derived, ultimately, from the Palaeo-Sinaitic
script with some influence from the Early Canaanite writing,

SOUTH-
SEMITIC
BRANCH

and that there may have been some *indirect* mutual influence
between it and its northern cousin; but that this picture is
subject to radical change when and if further relevant discoveries are made.

The offshoots from the South-Semitic branch included the
Minaean, Sabaean, Ḥimyaritic, Qatabanic, and Hadhra-
mautic scripts in southern Arabia; and the Thamudene, De-
danite, Liḥyanite and Ṣafaitic scripts in the northern part of the
Peninsula. The numerous inscriptions in these alphabetic forms
of writing are our principal source for the study of those flourishing kingdoms, including the Biblical Sheba, which were
relegated by the rise of Islam to the backwaters of history.

The Sabaean offshoot from the main branch of the South-
Semitic alphabet, a graceful, very elegant script consisting of
twenty-nine letters, spread into Africa. There it became the
progenitor of the Ethiopic alphabet, and this in turn gave birth
to the modern Amharic, Tigré, Tigriñya and other alphabets
of modern Ethiopia. These are the only South-Semitic
alphabetic scripts still in use today.

Fig. 27

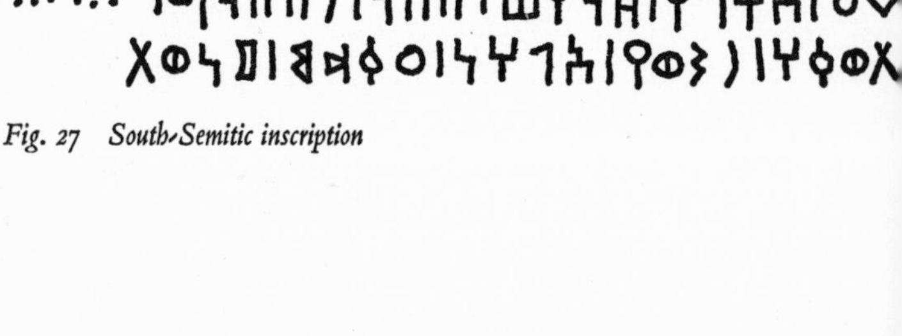

Fig. 27   *South-Semitic inscription*

Chapter VI

Diffusion of the Alphabet

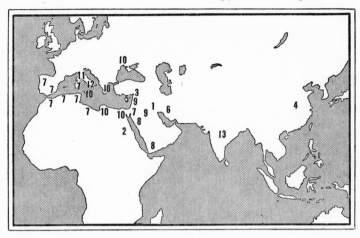

Fig. 28   Spread of the Alphabet c. 1000–1 B.C.

1, Cuneiform scripts; 2, Egyptian scripts; 3, Hittite hieroglyphics; 4, Chinese script; 5, Cyprus syllabary; 6, Persian semi-alphabetic cuneiform script; 7, Canaanite alpha- betic branch; 8, South-Semitic alphabetic branch; 9, Aramaic alphabetic branch; 10, Greek alphabet; 11, Etruscan alphabet; 12, Latin alphabet; 13, Indian branch

AT THE END OF THE SECOND millennium B.C., with the temporary or permanent eclipse of the Egyptians, Ba- bylonians, Assyrians, Hittites and Minoans, three nations of Syria and Palestine, at the geographical centre of the Fertile Crescent, acquired an increasing importance: Israel, Phoenicia and Aram. To the south of the Fertile Crescent the Sabaeans of the Arabian Peninsula attained a position of wealth and importance as commercial intermediaries between the Medi- terranean and the Far East. To the west, significant contact was established with the Greeks.

The rise of Israel, Phoenicia and Aram, together with the temporary elimination of foreign control such as was frequently

Fig. 28

Fig. 29

exercised over Syria and Palestine by the Egyptians or by the Mesopotamian peoples, favoured the spread of the new and revolutionary form of writing which, insofar as present evidence indicates, had been invented on Syrian or Palestinian soil. Within a comparatively short time, the North-Semitic alphabet had begun to branch out in a number of directions both on its 'home soil' and abroad. These branchings can most conveniently be illustrated by a simple diagram:

We shall examine in turn each of the offshoots from the North-Semitic Main Branch.

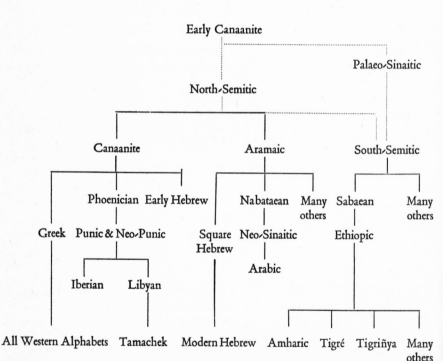

Fig. 29   North-Semitic and South-Semitic main branches, ... represents uncertainty of connection

CANAANITE BRANCH

The term 'Canaan' (Hebrew *Kena'an*, Egyptian hieroglyphic *K'ᐟnᐟn'*, cuneiform *Kiᐟnaᐟakhᐟkhi* or *Kiᐟnaᐟakhᐟna*, Greek and Latin *Chanaan*) appears in the Bible as the ancient name for Palestine. Conventionally, the 'Canaanites' are considered to have been the principal members of the second Semitic imᐟ migration into Palestine (beginning of the third millennium B.C.): the peoples who were partly extinguished and partly assimilated in the third Semitic invasion, which included the Hebrews and Aramaeans. From the philological point of view, 'Canaanite' is one of the two principal branches of the Northᐟ Semitic group of languages, the other being Araᐟ maic. On the basis of this latter definition the 'Canaanite' group includes the Hebrews and the Phoenicians, and, seᐟ condarily, such related peoples as the Moabites and Ammoᐟ nites. It is in this sense that we use the term 'Canaanite' here.

Very shortly after its appearance as a distinctive alphabetic script, the Canaanite offshoot from the Northᐟ Semitic Main Branch developed into two recognisably different ways of writing the same alphabet, namely the Early Hebrew, and the Phoenician.

(1) Early Hebrew: This term is used in contradistinction to the later 'Square Hebrew', an alphabet which was the parent of the classical Hebrew script. The Early Hebrew writing had already begun to acquire its distinctive character in the eleventh century B.C., and continued to be written (the shapes of the letters becoming progressively, though not strongly, modified) until the sixth century B.C., though it was used on a much diminished scale for several centuries after. To a large extent, the longᐟstanding paucity of Early Hebrew inscriptions has been broken in the past three decades, and today several

EARLY
HEBREW
ALPHABET

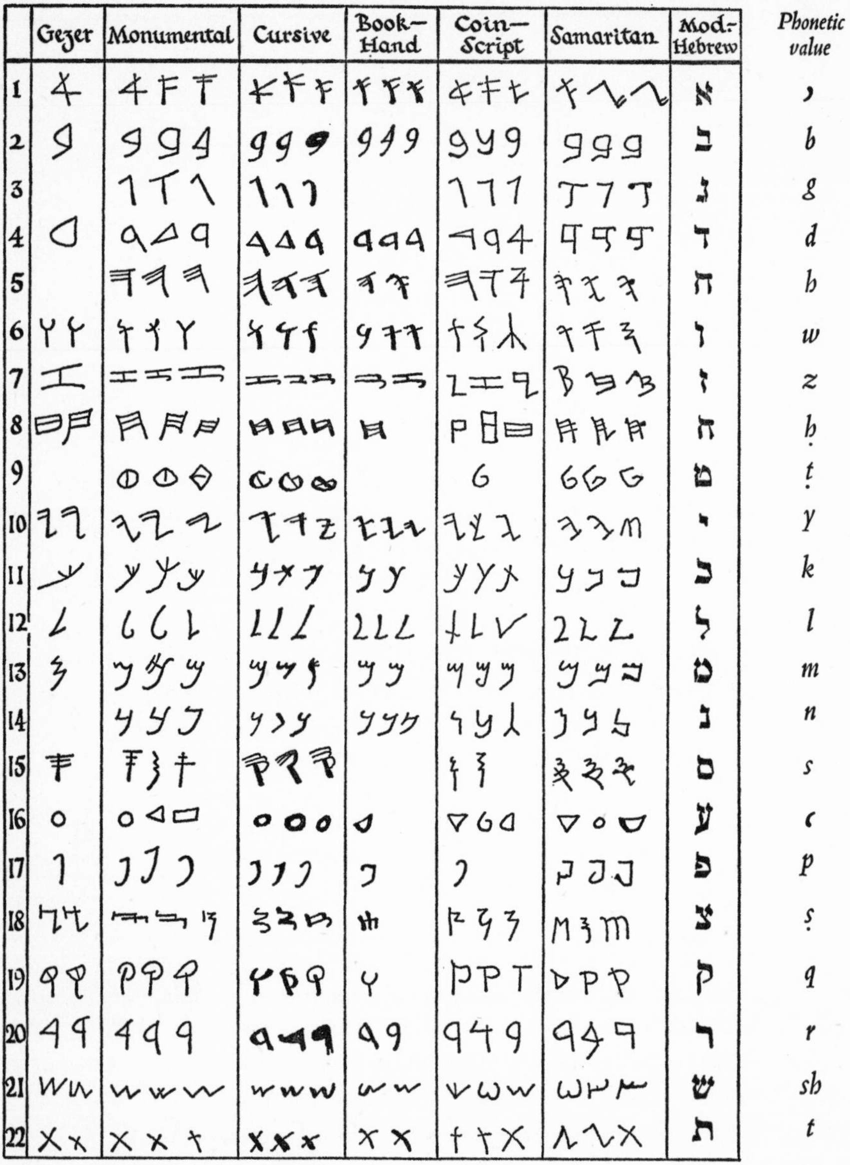
Gezer
Monumental
Cursive
Book-Hand
Coin-Script
Samaritan
Mod-Hebrew
Phonetic value
1 א ʼ
2 ב b
3 ג g
4 ד d
5 ה h
6 ו w
7 ז z
8 ח ḥ
9 ט ṭ
10 י y
11 כ k
12 ל l
13 מ m
14 נ n
15 ס s
16 ע ʻ
17 פ p
18 צ ṣ
19 ק q
20 ר r
21 ש sh
22 ת t

Fig. 30 Early Hebrew styles of writing

hundred such inscriptions can be listed. None of these can be said to deal with events of outstanding importance: yet they are of vital help in supplementing and illuminating the history, literature and language of the Old Testament.

The most ancient extant example of the Early Hebrew writing is the Gezer Calendar, which was inscribed with its bucolic ditty in the period of Saul or David (*c.* 1000 B.C. cf. page 114). Here we find the letters *kaph, mem, nun* and *pe* already marked by the Hebrew tendency to bend their main stems to the left. Nearing the eighth century B.C., the transformation to a quite distinctive Hebrew script becomes complete on *ostraca* (potsherds used as writing surfaces) from the Northern Kingdom. The same transformation is seen in somewhat later inscriptions from Judah, particularly the Siloam inscription (*c.* 700 B.C.) and the Lachish letters (*c.* 587 B.C.).

Several principal characteristics distinguish the Early Hebrew alphabet from the contemporary Phoenician manner of writing what was essentially the same script: (a) all the letters, but especially the *zayin* and the *sade*, are wider, shorter, more squat, and considerably more consistent and accurate; (b) the main stems of the letters *beth, kaph, lamed, mem, nun,* and *pe* are curved or rounded at the bottom, bending towards the left; (c) the vertical strokes of the *beth* extend beyond the horizontal ones; (d) the upper horizontal stroke of the *he* extends beyond the vertical; and (e) the short vertical strokes of the *mem* and *nun* are often not joined to the main stem. There are of course a good many variations from this pattern in the current hands of a particular period, especially in the Lachish letters of the sixth century B.C. (The Lachish letters, it may be added, represent the climax of the Early Hebrew cursive style. They are written in a beautiful flowing hand which confirms that the ancient Israelites could write with clarity and rapidity at one and the same time: a fact not without relevance in the study of some of the major Prophets.)

Fig. 31
Plate 46

Fig. 30

Plate 47

Figs 30–33
Plates 48, 49

Fig. 33

Fig. 31 Oldest extant example of the Early Hebrew ABC. The letters are from right to left)', b, g, d, h

The Early Hebrew writing had two descendants: the Samaritan script, and the writing used on Jewish coins from the Maccabaean period to the revolt of Bar-Kochba. It also influenced the Square Hebrew script from which the modern Hebrew writing is directly derived.

SAMARITAN
SCRIPT
Plate 52

The Samaritan script is the only direct descendant of the Early Hebrew writing which is still in use today. An attractive neat and symmetrical form of writing, it is employed by the few hundred Samaritans who represent all that remains of a once-flourishing religious sect.

JEWISH
COINS

The Early Hebrew script used on Jewish coins from 13? B.C. to A.D. 132-5 was already an archaic form when the earliest of these were minted. It was not, however, 'revived' (as we would say today) but had continued to be written, in a

Plates 50, 51

limited fashion, during the period when the Square Hebrew script was in common use.

EARLY
HEBREW
VERSUS
SQUARE
HEBREW

The Early Hebrew alphabet was employed as the common script of the Jews until the Babylonian Exile. The Hebrew script which came into use during the Babylonian period, and which was subsequently employed by the Jews who returned to Palestine, was essentially an adaptation of the Aramaic script, but one partly influenced by the Early Hebrew writing. A sepulchral inscription from 'Araq el-Emir (south-east of es Salt, in modern Jordan), dating from the late sixth or early fifth century B.C., may be said to represent a transitional stage between the Early Hebrew script and the *ketab meruba'*, or Square Hebrew writing.

A distinctive *Palestinian* Jewish version of the Square Hebrew script – as distinguished from that used by Jewish communities elsewhere – has been traced from the third century B.C. It became a standardised form towards the end of the first century B.C.; and it was from this script that the modern Hebrew writing developed over a period of two millennia.

(2) Phoenician: It is difficult to overestimate the importance

Fig. 32 Early Hebrew alphabet: 'royal' jar-handle stamp of the seventh century B.C. The inscription reads (from right to left): top, l m l k ('to the Ring', 'royal') and, bottom, h b r n ('Hebron': the city of Hebron

	I	II	III	IV	V	VI	Phonetic value
א							ʾ
ב							b
ג							g
ד							d
ה							h
ו							w
ז							z
ח							ḥ
ט							ṭ
י							y
כ							k
ל							l
מ							m
נ							n
ס							s
ע							ʿ
פ							p
צ							ṣ
ק							q
ר							r
ש							sh
ת							t

Fig. 33 Early Hebrew: main styles of the Lachish Letters, representing the climax of the Early Hebrew cursive style of writing

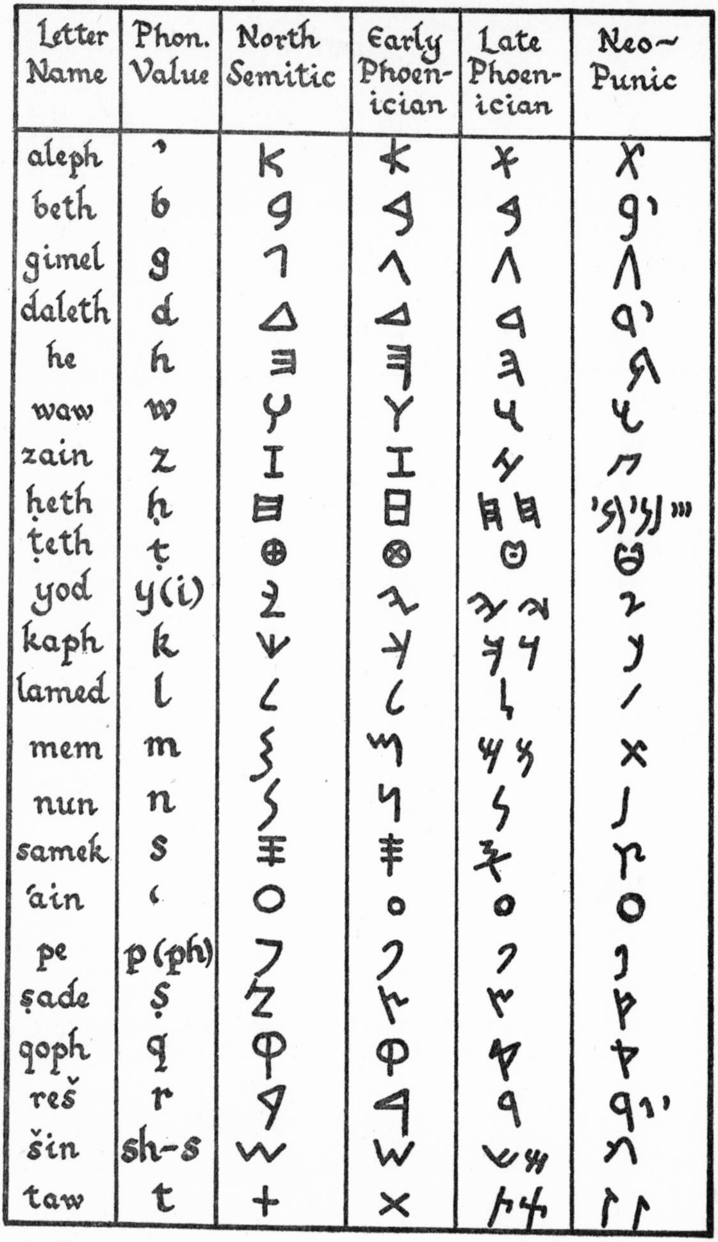

Letter Name	Phon. Value	North Semitic	Early Phoenician	Late Phoenician	Neo-Punic
aleph	ʾ				
beth	b				
gimel	g				
daleth	d				
he	h				
waw	w				
zain	z				
ḥeth	ḥ				
ṭeth	ṭ				
yod	y(i)				
kaph	k				
lamed	l				
mem	m				
nun	n				
samek	s				
ʿain	ʿ				
pe	p (ph)				
ṣade	ṣ				
qoph	q				
reš	r				
šin	sh–s				
taw	t				

Fig. 34 Phoenician alphabetic branch

of the Phoenician alphabetic script in the history of writing. PHOENICIAN
ALPHABET
Fig. 34
Through its adoption and adaptation by the Greeks it became
the direct ancestor of all Western alphabetic writings. In its
own right it was an important (perhaps a vital) adjunct of a
trading system which extended from the coast of Palestine to
the Straits of Gibraltar, and which spanned a period of well
over a millennium.

The earliest definitely readable inscription in the North-
Semitic alphabet is the Akhiram epitaph, found at Byblos in Plate 36
Phoenicia, which probably dates from the eleventh century
B.C. There is no doubt that Phoenician use of the North-
Semitic alphabet went back further than this, but a lack of
inscriptions renders its earlier history conjectural. Moreover,
between the earliest extant inscriptions found in Phoenicia itself,
all of which date from the eleventh and tenth centuries B.C., Plates 37, 38
Plate 39
and the indigenous Phoenician inscriptions of the Helenistic
period, there is a total (and unexplained) gap.

The rarity of indigenous documents stands in contrast to
the numbers of Phoenician inscriptions found elsewhere.
Examples of Early Hebrew writing have been found almost
exclusively within the boundaries of Palestine; but Phoenician
inscriptions have been discovered on Cyprus, Malta, Sicily
and Sardinia, and in Greece, North Africa, Marseilles, Spain,
and eastern Cilicia: to wit, throughout the vast trading and
colonial empire of this singularly industrious and adventurous
people.

Three principal subdivisions of the Phoenician script can
be traced, the first of which is the Phoenician script proper.
It was used on the mainland of Phoenicia down to the second
or first century B.C.

The second is the Phoenician colonial branch, of which at
least three varieties can be distinguished on the basis of extant
archaeological evidence: (a) the Cypro-Phoenician script used
from approximately the tenth to the second century B.C.; (b)

Plates 40, 41

Plates 42–45

the Sardinian, represented by the Nora Stone and two fragmentary inscriptions, all of which can be dated in the early
ninth century B.C.; and (c) the Carthaginian, which subsequently attained such importance in its own right that it shall
be treated as the third major subdivision of the Phoenician
script.

The Carthaginian (or Punic) alphabetic writing was of two
types, monumental and cursive, and had as a direct offshoot
the more cursive form known as neo-Punic. The last Carthaginian (neo-Punic) inscription we know of belongs to the
third century A.D., indicating that in this case the daughter (or
granddaughter) script survived its parent by some five centuries. Two scripts were either derived from or at least strongly
influenced by, the Carthaginian writing: (1) the early Libyan
(or Numidian) writing used by the ancestors of the Berbers;
(2) the Iberian scripts dating from the fifth to the first century
B.C. The Libyan script was in its turn the progenitor of the
Tamachek writing still in use today among the Tuareg of
north-west Africa. Bi-lingual inscriptions from the Roman
period exist which include such combinations as Libyan-
Punic or Libyan-neo-Punic, and Libyan-Latin.

The Phoenician alphabet in all its subdivisions (including
Punic and neo-Punic), like the Early Hebrew alphabet, underwent a development which was in essence purely external: the
total number of letters, and their phonetic values, remained the
same; the writing consistently runs from right to left. The most
distinctive external change in the shapes of the Phoenician
letters was that, through the centuries, they came to be written
in an increasingly thin and elongated form; whereas in the
Early Hebrew script, as we have seen, they became progressively
shorter and thicker.

As a third category, it remains to mention a number of
secondary offshoots from the Canaanite branch, contemporary
with, and closely resembling, the Early Hebrew script.

The most dramatically documented of these is the Moabite writing, even though only three Moabite inscriptions remain: for while two of these are only inscribed seals the third is the famous *stele* of Mesha', King of Moab, in which he celebrates his triumph over Israel after the fall of the Omriad dynasty (cf. 2 *Kings* iii, 4–27, where a rather different account of the same conflict is given). The *stele* belongs to the middle of the ninth century B.C.

Of the Edomite writing only two inscriptions have been found, but these are of the highest interest. The first was discov‚ ered in 1938 by the American archaeologist N. Glueck at Tell el‚Kheleifeh on the northern coast of the Gulf of Aqabah: six characters incised on a jug after firing. The jug was found in a room attributed to the eighth or seventh century B.C. Of the letters, one is damaged and another uncertain.

The second and even more interesting discovery was made at the same site: twelve stamped jar‚handles, all apparently impressed with the same small seal. The inscription reads (in two lines) *l Qws'nl/'bd hmlk*: that is, '[belonging] to *Qws'nl*, the servant of the King'. This high official of the Edomite king had a theophorous name beginning with the element *Qws* (probably pronounced *Qôs* or *Qaus*), the title of the chief Edomite deity. The lettering of this inscription strongly resem‚ bles that on the jug. Both inscriptions have been dated in the seventh century B.C.

Three seals inscribed in the Ammonite script have come down to us. It, too, strongly resembles the Early Hebrew alphabet.

ARAMAIC BRANCH

In the twelfth and eleventh centuries B.C., with the gradual decline as political powers of Egypt, Assyria, the Hittites and Minoan Crete, the Aramaean tribes who had entered

northern Syria as part of the third Semitic immigration suc‑
ceeded, by force of arms and numbers, in establishing a chain
of petty kingdoms throughout the most favourable lands of
northern and southern Mesopotamia, and Syria. The most
important of these was *Aram Dammesheq* (Damascus), usually
referred to simply as *Aram*, followed by *Aram Naharaim* and
Sam'al. For three centuries these little states remained in a state
of uneasy coexistence, forming defensive unions when neces‑
sary and warring among themselves when outside pressures
were removed. None attained sufficient strength to assert com‑
plete supremacy over the others.

In the ninth century B.C. the Assyrian king Tukulti‑Ninurta
II (889–884 B.C.) began the slow process of Assyrian recovery.
For a century thereafter yearly campaigns succeeded in re‑
establishing Assyrian hegemony over a good part of the Near
East. One after another, the Aramaean states gave way under
Assyrian onslaught. The last survivor, Damascus, fell in 732
B.C.

But the end of Aramaean political independence was by no
means the end of Aramaean history. On the contrary, it marked
the beginning of Aramaean cultural and economic supremacy
in western Asia. The transplantation of masses of Aramaeans
by the Assyrians, a political measure to break up military
DIFFUSION   aliances, bore remarkable fruit. By the end of the eight century
OF ARAMAIC   B.C. the use of the Aramaic language and alphabet had become
LANGUAGE   very widespread in Assyria itself; by the end of the following
AND SCRIPT   century all Syria and a large part of Mesopotamia had become
thoroughly Aramaised. Aramaic became the *lingua franca* of
the Near East, as Akkadian had been in an earlier epoch.

Under the Achaemenidae of Persia it became the Empire's
diplomatic language, and the principal speech of traders from
Egypt and Asia Minor to India. Such was the vitality of this
language that it was used for more than a thousand years after
the political decay of the Aramaeans. The various languages

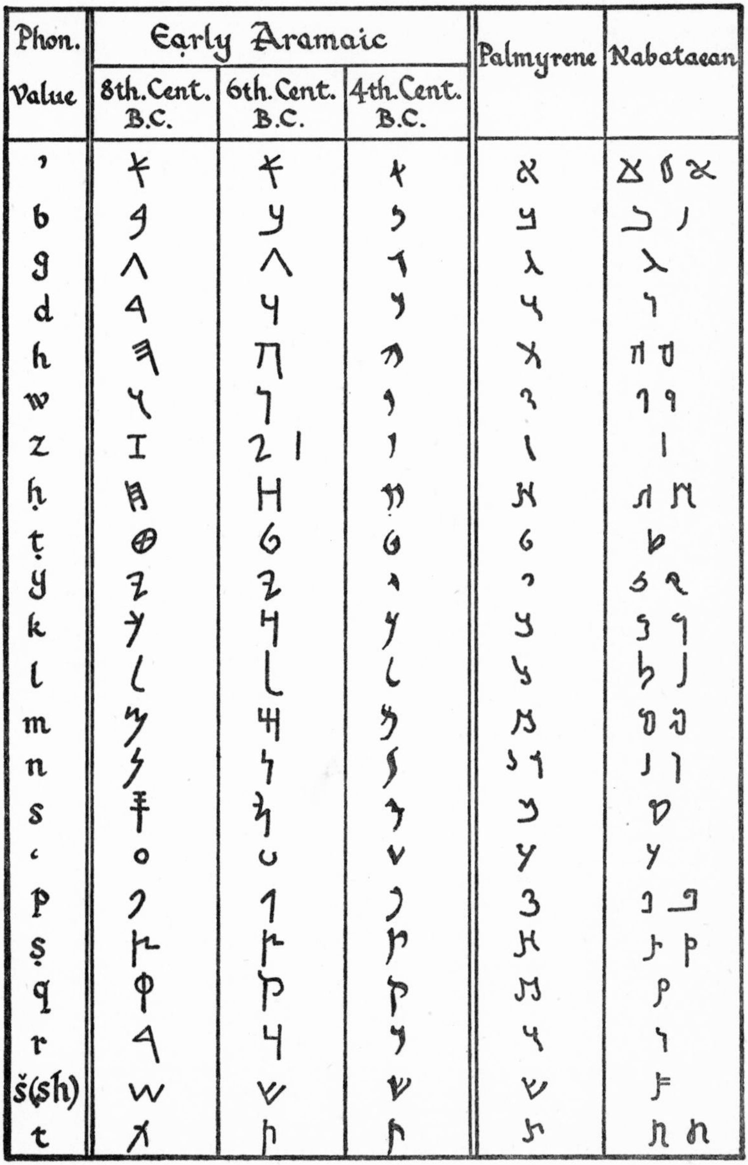

Phon. Value	Early Aramaic			Palmyrene	Nabataean
	8th. Cent. B.C.	6th. Cent. B.C.	4th. Cent. B.C.		
'					
b					
g					
d					
h					
w					
z					
ḥ					
ṭ					
y					
k					
l					
m					
n					
s					
ʿ					
p					
ṣ					
q					
r					
š (sh)					
t					

Fig. 35
Aramaic
alphabetic
branch

135

and dialects descended from it flourished for many centuries more. For over a thousand years it was the vernacular speech of the Jews, and took a place beside Hebrew in their religious and literary life. It was the language spoken by Jesus and the Apostles, and probably the original language of the Gospels as well. Only the unifying force of Islam, carrying with it the Arabic alphabet and language, finally brought Aramaic to virtual extinction.

The adaptation of the North-Semitic Alphabet to the Aramaic language took place at some time in the tenth or early ninth century B.C. The earliest Aramaic inscription of any importance found so far, a fragment of a royal *stele*, has been dated at approximately 850 B.C. It includes the name of the Aramaean king Ben-Hadad of Damascus. This is followed in time by the *stele* of Zakir, king of Ḥamath and Lu'ash, attributed to about 775 B.C.

On the whole, the few early Aramaic inscriptions which have been found until now belong to the ninth, eighth and seventh centuries B.C. Inscriptions from the sixth and later centuries are far larger in number, and this increase reflects the

Plate 53

rapid spread of the script throughout the Near East. Numerous Aramaic papyri and *ostraca* have been found in Egypt: the earliest of these can be dated at about 515 B.C., while the most famous are the Elephantine papyri, containing information of a religious and economic nature about a fifth-century Jewish military colony in Egypt. The succeeding centuries are bridged

Fig. 36 (opposite) Development of Square Hebrew alphabet. In the more than bimillennial development of the Hebrew alphabet three fundamental types can be traced: (a) Square Hebrew, which evolved into the neat, well-proportioned printing type of modern Hebrew; the majority of the 'Dead Sea Scrolls' (the most famous and most controversial discovery of the last fifteen years) are in the Square Hebrew script; (b) rabbinic, also known as Rashi-writing, which was the mediaeval book- or literary hand; and (c) cursive script, which gave rise to many local varieties (Oriental, Spanish, Italian, Franco-German, and so on), of which the Polish-German form became the Hebrew cursive script of today

	Square Hebrew [Monumental]	Medieval Formal Styles	Rabbinic Styles	Cursive Styles	Contemporary	
					Cursive	Print
1						א
2						ב
3						ג
4						ד
5						ה
6						ו
7						ז
8						ח
9						ט
10						י
11						כ ך
12						ל
13						מ ם
14						נ ן
15						ס
16						ע
17						פ ף
18						צ ץ
19						ק
20						ר
21						ש
22						ת

by an Aramaic inscription from Taima, in northern Arabi (fifth century); Aramaic *ostraca* discovered by N. Glueck a Tell el-Kheleifeh, ranging from the sixth to the fourth centur B.C.; and a third century inscription found at Taxila in north western India.

As this amazing geographical range confirms, the Aramai writing became, in the second half of the first millennium B.C. the most important and widespread script of the Near East winning its prolonged 'duel' with cuneiform, and establishing in place of complicated theocratic writings accessible only to few privileged classes, what we may call, without too muc distortion, a democratic script.

An interesting parallel with the Phoenician writing is th fact that only a very few Aramaic inscriptions have been foun in Aram itself, and none for the period after the sixth centur B.C. The most important Aramaic documents have been foun in Lycia, Cappadocia, Lydia, Cilicia, Assyria, northern Ara bia and (especially) Egypt. Others have been discovered as fa afield as Greece, Afghanistan and India.

At the time of its adoption the Aramaic script was of cours very little different from those descendants of the North-Semiti alphabet originally used by the Hebrews and Phoenicians Gradually, however, it too assumed a distinctive character, an was marked by four principal tendencies: (1) the opening o the tops and sides of the letters *beth*, *daleth*, *resh* and *'ayin*; (2) th progressive reduction of the number of separate strokes use for such letters as *heth* and *teth*; (3) a rounding-off of shar angles in the letters; and (4) the introduction of ligatures. Pro gressive modification of this sort began in the seventh and con tinued into the early fifth century B.C.

OFFSHOOTS
FROM THE
ARAMAIC
SCRIPT

When we come to examine the offshoots from the Aramai script we are confronted with the curious fact that while th Phoenician alphabet was the ancestor of all the alphabeti writings west of Syria, the Aramaic alphabet moved in a dia

צדה צלעתה

Fig. 37 Hebrew portion of the inscription on the sarcophagus of Queen Ṣarah-Helena of Adiabene, from the 'Tomb of the Kings', Jerusalem. The only early Square Hebrew inscription that can be dated with reasonable accuracy (A.D. 50–60)

Fig 38 Babylonian bowl with magical inscription in Square Hebrew. (Eighth century A.D.)

Fig. 35

metrically opposite direction and became the progenitor of the hundreds of alphabetic writings used, at various times, in the East. The direct and indirect descendants of the Aramaic script can be divided into two principal categories: (1) scripts employed for Semitic languages, and (2) writings adapted to non-Semitic tongues.

Figs. 36–38

Plate 60

The first of these categories can be broken down into (a) Square Hebrew, (b) Nabataean-Neo-Sinaitic-Arabic, (c) Palmyrene, (d) Syriac-Nestorian, (e) Mandaean, and (f) Manichaean. Each of these scripts had a fascinating and sometimes chequered history of its own, but we have space here to consider only the three writings under (b).

NABATEAN
ALPHABET

The Nabataeans were an Arabic people, speaking Arabic in daily life, who used Aramaic as their written language, adopting for literary purposes not only the Aramaic alphabet but the tongue itself. Their kingdom of Petra, located between modern Jordan, northern Arabia and Sinai, stood for four centuries, from the second century B.C. to the second century A.D.: but even before that time a Nabataean tribe had been powerful enough (in 312-311 B.C.) to gain a victory against Antigonus, one of the inheritors of Alexander the Great. For a short time they exercised hegemony over all the territory from the Euphrates to the Red Sea and down to the centre of the Arabian Peninsula. In 85 B.C. they occupied Damascus. But in A.D. 106 the kingdom of Petra lost its independence and became the Arabian Province of the Roman Empire, with Bosra as its capital.

The Nabataean descendant of the Aramaic script can be traced from the late second century B.C., though it did not assume a truly distinctive character until after the middle of the first century B.C. It became a standardised form at the beginning of the first century A.D. After the dissolution of the Nabataean kingdom by the Romans the script gradually ceased to be written.

At some time before A.D. 106, however, the Nabataean script had become the parent of an offshoot known as Neo- Sinaitic (to distinguish it from the Palaeo-Sinaitic inscrip- tions, which we have already discussed). A more cursive form than the Nabataean writing, Neo-Sinaitic has been found prin- cipally in the form of short rock-inscriptions in the Sinai Pen- insula, and particularly in the Wady Mukattab ('Valley of the Writings'), about seventy-five miles from Suez. These con- sist largely of names and votive scribblings. They are of little importance except insofar as the Neo-Sinaitic script is the probable link between the Nabataean and Arabic alphabets.

After the Latin alphabet the Arabic script is the most widely- used form of alphabetic writing in the modern world. The Arab conquests of the seventh and eighth centuries A.D., carry- ing with them the religion of Islam and the Koran, brought the Arabic language and script to the vast expanse of territory which extends from India to the Atlantic Ocean.

The Arabic script spread even further than the language itself. It became in turn the official writing of the Persian and Ottoman empires; it was carried to south-eastern Russia, and to western, central and south-eastern Asia; it spread over a good part of Africa. The Arabic alphabet was adapted, generally with some necessary modification, to such diverse languages as Slavonic, Spanish, Persian, Hindustani, Turkish, Hebrew, Berber, Swahili, Sudanese, and others. It drove out of use a number of scripts derived from the Syriac alphabet, as well as the Coptic and the Persian writings. It 'expelled' the Greek alphabet from Anatolia, Syria and Egypt, the Latin alphabet from North Africa, and the Cyrillic script from Bosnia. Although many Arabic dialects developed and radically di- verged from one another, the written language has invariably conformed to the type called 'classical Arabic'. The latter has an enormously rich vocabulary and a great variety of grammatical forms.

The most likely conjecture which can at present be enter-
tained is that the Arabic alphabet originated at some time in
the fourth century A.D., in a direct line of descent, through the
Neo-Sinaitic script, from that of the Nabataeans. The earliest
extant Arabic writing is a trilingual inscription (Greek-Syriac-
Arabic) of A.D. 512. But the precise origins of the Arabic
script and its early history remain obscure. All that can be said
with certainty is that from a very early time the manner in
which the script varied was not only geographical but stylistic.

The tenth-century Arab writer Nadim of Baghdad distinguished two principal early branches of Arabic writing – the
style of Mecca and Medina, and the style of Basra and Kufa.
The first of these had, according to Nadim, three sub-varieties;
the second, six. He also distinguished three varieties of the
somewhat later Isfahani branch, one of which, the *qairamuz*,
became the prototype of the Persian Arabic script. It is certain
that Nadim was reliable at least in part, but most of his classifications remain unverified by documentary evidence.

The two principal types of Arabic writing which developed
in the early Mohammedan period were the *Kufic* (from the
town of Kufa in Mesopotamia, seat of a famous Moslem academy), and the *Naskhi* (or Mecca-Medina). A heavy, bold and

Plates 55, 56

lapidary style, Kufic appeared towards the end of the seventh
century A.D. It was particularly suitable for writing on stone
and metal, for painted or carved inscriptions on the walls of
mosques, and for the lettering on coins. Nevertheless, it was
also used for writing manuscripts of the Koran, many of which
are extant today. The letters in Kufic are generally thick, squat
and upright; with the high development of Arabic calligraphy
it became an exceptionally beautiful script. From it were
derived a number of other script-forms, chiefly medieval, in
North and Central Africa, Spain and northern Arabia. Thereafter it was virtually discontinued except for such purposes as
could only be served by a formal and monumental writing.

Plates 57–59

The Naskhi writing was from the very outset a more cursive form, and was always chiefly employed for writing on papyrus. Nadim (*see* above) listed its three principal characteristics: (a) the *alif* bends to the right; (b) the upright strokes of the letters are somewhat elongated; (c) the script as a whole slants slightly toward the left. In the course of time the Naskhi script became the parent of innumerable styles and varieties including the *ta'liq* (with its seventy or so secondary forms), the *ryq'a* (the most commonly-used script of the Ottoman Empire), the *diwani* (used for official Turkish documents), the *thülüth* (ornamental) and the *syakat* (used principally by the Janissaries). The Naskhi became the direct ancestor of the modern Arabic writing.

Like other Semitic scripts, Arabic is written from right to left. The Arabic alphabet consists of twenty-eight consonantal letters, twenty-two being directly derived from the Aramaic-Nabataean branch of the old Semitic alphabet, and six being new additions. Although for many centuries the sequence of letters exactly followed the older Semitic pattern (the six added consonants being placed at the end in any listing of all the characters), significant divergencies were present from the very outset in the shapes and grammatical values of the different signs. Indeed, no branch of the Aramaic alphabet underwent so rapid an evolution in the externals of shape and form as the Nabataean-Neo-Sinaitic-Arabic. And the necessities of adapting the older form to the distinctive Arabic speech caused a number of significant changes to be made: (a) the addition of the letters *tha, dhal, za, dad, kha* (like Scottish *ch*) and *ghain* (uvular *r*); (b) a consequent rearrangement of the letters in their new grammatical order which is followed in modern Arabic vocabularies and grammars, the order being *'alif, ba, ta, tha, jim, ha, kha, dal, dhal, ra, za, sin, shin, sad, dad, ta, za, 'ayin, ghain, fa, qaf, kaf, lam, mim, nun, ha, waw, ya*. All these letters represent consonants; three of them, *alif, waw* and *ya*, are used as long

CHARACTERISTICS OF ARABIC WRITING

vowels. To the twenty-eight letters we have listed may be added the *hamza*, or glottal stop: a click produced by a quick compression of the upper part of the throat.

The written letters undergo a slight external change according to their position within a word. When they stand alone or come at the end of a word, they ordinarily terminate in a bold stroke; when they appear in the middle of a word, they are ordinarily joined to the letter following by a small upward curve. With the exception of six letters which can only be joined to *preceding* letters, the initial and medial forms of the characters are much abbreviated while the final form consists of the initial form together with a triumphant flourish. In manuscripts and expensively-printed books the letters are often beautifully interwoven through ligatures.

The use of diacritical marks (including signs for short vowels, which are sometimes used in conjunction with the letters *alif*, *waw* and *ya*) was introduced in Basra in the early eighth century A.D., and was probably borrowed from the Syriac script. In addition to providing vowel-sounds they distinguish different consonants.

ADAPTATION OF THE ARAMAIC ALPHABET TO NON-SEMITIC LANGUAGES

It remains to mention, with necessary brevity, the most important adaptations of the Aramaic alphabet (through some of its major offshoots) to the writing of non-Semitic languages.

INDIAN SCRIPTS
Fig. 39

The Aramaic alphabet was probably the prototype of the Brahmi script of India; the latter was the parent of nearly all Indian scripts down to the present time. The transmission took place, in all probability, at some time in the seventh century B.C.; and it is possible that the agents who effected it were Semitic merchants for whom Aramaic was a native tongue and script. (The presence of Aramaic-writing men in India in a somewhat later period is attested by the Aramaic inscriptions found at Taxila on the Hydaspes and elsewhere. It is safe to assume that commercial relations between Semitic and Indo-Aryan merchants began at a much earlier time.)

The adaptation of the Aramaic script to the Indo-Aryan language was by no means simple or straightforward. The shapes of many of the Brahmi letters show clear Semitic influence, and the Brahmi script was originally written from right to left: but we must say that on the whole it was the *idea* of alphabetic writing which was transmitted, and that the fully-developed Brahmi system was the outcome more of brilliant philological and phonological elaboration than of direct borrowing.

At some time in the fifth century B.C., the second of the prototypal Indian alphabets – the Kharoshthi script – came into being in north-western India, which was at that time under Persian rule. It was definitely derived from the Aramaic script. The Persian influence made this a more direct process than in the origin of the Brahmi writing, and one which has undergone less dispute in scholarly circles. Unlike the Brahmi script, the Kharoshthi's influence – if any – on other scripts seems to have been negligible. Indeed, it was itself influenced by the Brahmi in its origin and evolution.

In the later centuries of its existence the Brahmi script gave birth to a number of types or varieties of which Buehler, the greatest authority on the subject, listed eight. They cannot here be discussed in detail, but we may note that three of them – the early and late Maurya type, and the Śuṅga variety – became, in the first centuries B.C. and A.D., the prototypes of what is usually referred to as the North Indian subdivision of the Brahmi script. Out of this subdivision arose the monumental form of writing known as Gupta which was employed from the fourth through the sixth century A.D., and which became the ancestor of the great majority of Indian scripts. The western variety of the Gupta writing spread into Eastern (or Chinese) Turkestan – where it was used to represent a number of languages (including the recently discovered Agnean and Ku-chean dialects, also called, though wrongly, Tokharian A and

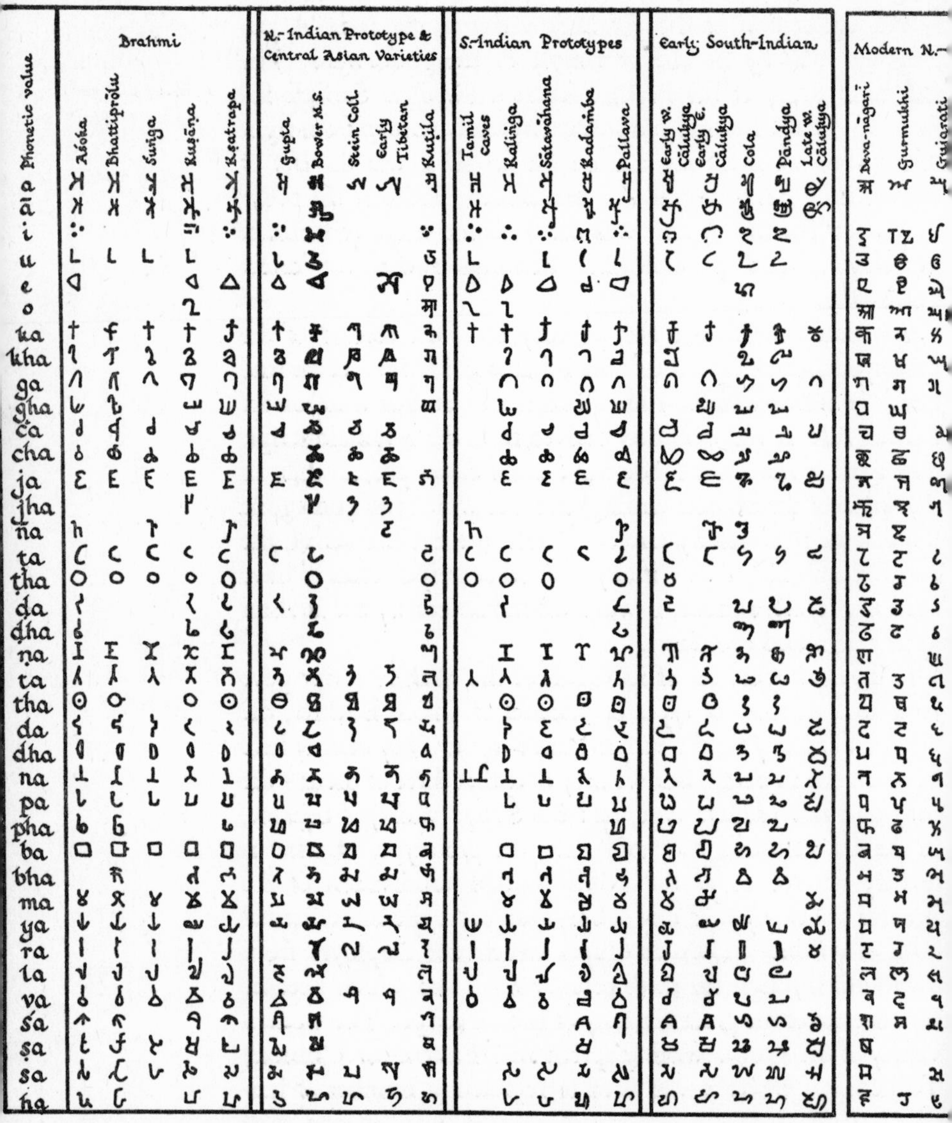
Phonetic value
Brahmi
Aśoka
Bhattiprōlu
Śuṅga
Kuṣāṇa
Kṣatrapa
N.-Indian Prototype & Central Asian Varieties
Gupta
Bower M.S.
Stein Coll.
Early Tibetan
Kuṭila
S.-Indian Prototypes
Tamil Caves
Kaliṅga
Sātavāhana
Kadamba
Pallava
Early South-Indian
Early W. Cālukya
Early E. Cālukya
Cola
Pāṇḍya
Late W. Cālukya
Modern N.-
Deva-nāgarī
Gurmukhi
Gujarati
a
ā
i
u
e
o
ka
kha
ga
gha
ca
cha
ja
jha
ña
ṭa
ṭha
ḍa
ḍha
ṇa
ta
tha
da
dha
na
pa
pha
ba
bha
ma
ya
ra
la
va
śa
ṣa
sa
ha

Fig. 39 Development of the main Indian alphabets from the third century B.C. onwards

South-Indian						(Further-Indian) Sinhalese				Further-Indian		Further Indian									
Vijayanagar	Telugu	Kanarese	Grantha	Tamil	Vatteluttu	Vessagiri (a)	Mahāratmale	Vessagiri (b)	Modern	Vō-Cạnh	Pūrṇavarma	Mon	Pyu	(Burmese) Kyok-cha	(Burmese) Pali	(Burmese) cha-lonh	Patimokha	Modern Siamese	Ahom	Erlanga	Modern Javanese

B) – and strongly influenced the invention of the Tibetan script (A.D. 639).

But long before the rise of the Gupta empire, the Brahmi script had already begun its eastward movement. The Indo-Aryan migration to Ceylon in the fifth century B.C. had set the stage there: and the earliest Brahmi inscriptions in Ceylon can be dated in the third century B.C. Most dramatic of all, however, was the rise of Buddhism in India and its consequent expansion from India into Burma, Thailand, Cambodia, Laos, Vietnam, Malaya and Indonesia. Unlike the conquests of Islam, this was a peaceful movement. Its 'soldiers' were Buddhist monks who built an empire founded, not on political or military domination, but on the cultural and spiritual com-munity of peoples who were politically more or less indepen-dent of each other. Among many other achievements these monks brought offshoots from the Brahmi script, principally from its South Indian varieties, into being throughout all the vast extent of territory from India itself to the Philippines. And each of these scripts – from the Cham writing of Cambodia to the Kavi character of Java and its Sumatran offshoots, and the Tagalog writing of the Philippines – had as its ultimate ancestor the adapted script of a minor Semitic people, living in Syria and Mesopotamia, who disappeared politically in the eighth century B.C.

OTHER NON-
SEMITIC
OFFSHOOTS
OF ARAMAIC
Plate 54

Some of the other scripts which were directly or indirectly adapted from the Aramaic alphabet to the non-Semitic lan-guages of Central, South and South-East Asia are: (1) the Persian (or Iranian) scripts known as Pahlavi, which were chiefly used for writing the sacred (pre-Islamic) Persian litera-ture; (2) Sogdian, a language and script which constituted the *lingua franca* of Central Asia in the second half of the first millennium A.D.; (3) Kök Turki, a script used from the sixth to the eighth century A.D. by Turkish tribes living in the southern part of central Siberia, in north-western Mongolia, and in north-eastern Turkestan (from it was descended the early Hungarian alphabet); (4) the script of the Uighurs, a Turkic-speaking people who lived in Mongolia and eastern Turkestan – in the early thirteenth century this script was adapted, with Tibetan influence, as the writing of the Mongol Empire, the so-called Kalika script; (5) the early scripts of the Mongols, including Kalmuk, Buriat, Mongolian proper, and the allied Manchu writing; (6) the Armenian and Georgian scripts created by St Mesrop in the early fifth century A.D.

Plate 61

GREEK ALPHABET

In the history of alphabetic writing in the West, as in so many other fields, the Greeks are of paramount importance. The script adapted by them from the Semites was the direct or indirect ancestor of all the alphabetic scripts commonly used in Europe today; and although it was an adaptation rather than an invention, they improved it to such an extent that it has remained for three thousand years, with only slight modifica-tions, an unexampled vehicle of expression and communica-tion for men of the most diverse nationalities and tongues.

That the Greek alphabet was in fact directly adapted from that of the Semites is now thought by all serious scholars. That the adaptation took place in the tenth or ninth century B.C. is more and more the accepted view, though scholarly dispute on this subject, complicated by an almost total lack of positive evidence, remains intense. It is worth adding that no evidence has hitherto been found for writing of any kind in Greece between the Linear B Pylos tablets of *c.* 1200 B.C. and the taking-over of the Semitic alphabet.

Like most Semitic alphabetic scripts the earliest Greek alpha-betic writing was written from right to left, succeeded (in the sixth century B.C.) by *boustrophedon*, each of these styles being written in horizontal lines which occasionally ran from the bot-

Fig. 40

149

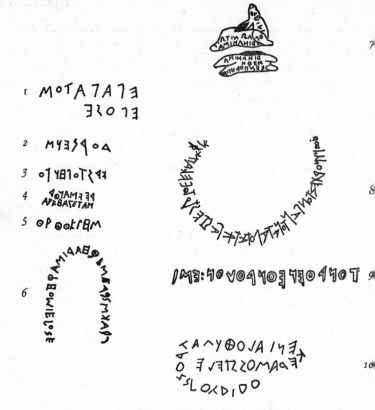

Fig. 40 Early Greek inscriptions written from right to left: 1–6, inscriptions from Thera; 7, Ionic votive inscription to Apollo; 8–10, inscriptions from Athens

tom to the top of the writing surface. A few early inscriptions are extant in which the writing runs from left to right. After approximately 500 B.C., left to right and top to bottom were the invariable directions followed by Greek inscriptions.

When the Alphabet was first adapted by the Greek the let-ters *beth, gimel, daleth, zayin, kaph, lamed, mem, nun, pe, resh* and *taw* (to give them their Semitic names) were taken over without change in their phonetic values, since they expressed sounds

Early Greek Alphabets 8th.—7th.cent.B.C.

Fig. 41   Early Greek alphabets

common to both the Semitic and Greek languages. The principal changes made were as follows: (1) a revolutionary transformation of the Semitic letters *aleph, he, waw, yod* and *'ayin* into the vowels *alpha, epsilon, upsilon, iota* and *omikron;* (2) a rearrangement of the sibilant sounds, of which the Semitic alphabets had a considerable variety; (3) the invention of sym-bols to represent sounds of the Greek language which were not even approximately expressed by any of the Semitic letters, i.e. *ph, ps, kh* and *x;* (4) the adoption of some Semitic letters for slightly different Greek sounds: *teth* (hard *t*) for *th*, a secondary form of *waw* for *digamma*, and *qoph* (emphatic *k*) for *koppa* (a form which was differentiated from *kappa*, but which dis-appeared from the eastern Greek alphabets by the fifth century B.C., surviving in the west as the numeral 90).

SUBDIVISION
OF GREEK
ALPHABET
Fig. 41

The eastern and western subdivisions were the two principal branches of the early Greek alphabet. The Ionic alphabet was the most important of the former, which also included the scripts of Asia Minor and the adjacent islands, of the Cyclades and Attica, of Sicyon and Argos, and of Megara, Corinth and the Ionian colonies of Magna Graecia. A secondary branch of the eastern subdivision was made up of the alphabets used on the Dorian islands of Thera, Melos and Crete.

The differences between the two subdivisions were variations in detail and not of essential structure. Thus, in the western alphabets, which had adopted the Semitic *heth* (a guttural breathing sound) to denote the Greek *spiritus asper* (a breathing sound of a somewhat softer kind), the Semitic *he* was used for both the long and the short *e* of the Greek language; while in most of the eastern alphabets, *he* came to represent the short *e* only, *heth* being used for the long *e*.

It is a controversial point whether the eastern or the western branch of the Greek alphabet was the earlier in time. Indeed, we cannot be completely certain that there was any derivative link between one and the other, and that they do not represent two quite independent adaptations of the Semitic alphabet, though it is more probable that both derive from a single earlier prototype. Some scholars consider the Ionic alphabet to be the earliest. Others hold that the western branch preceded the eastern. There is at least a possibility that the very early alphabet of the island of Thera was the prototype of all the rest.

Despite their original variations the local Greek alphabets gradually moved in the direction of uniformity. In 403 B.C. the Ionic alphabet of Miletus was officially adopted at Athens, and in the following half-century this action was followed by the other mainland states as well. By the middle of the fourth century B.C. almost all the local alphabets had been replaced by the Ionic, which thus became the established, classical Greek script of twenty-four letters.

After this time the development of the Greek alphabet was almost wholly external, in the direction of greater utility, convenience, and, above all, beauty. The classical style was retained as a monumental script at the same time that more cursive forms grew up for writing on such surfaces as parchment, papyrus and wax. In the middle of the third century B.C. Aristophanes of Byzantium introduced the three accents – acute, grave and circumflex – which were thereafter used to assist students (particularly foreigners) in the correct pronunciation of the words: these continue to be used in most Greek texts printed today. It is important to remember, of course, that they were originally meant to mark tone or pitch and not stress.

Countless inscriptions have been discovered in all parts of what was once the Hellenic and Hellenistic world; so many that a brief catalogue would be useless and misleading. Suffice it to say that they include official decrees (like the recently-discovered decree of Themistocles, a direct copy of that issued shortly before Salamis), annals, law-codes, civic rolls, temple accounts, votive offerings, *ostraca*, sepulchral inscriptions, coins, lettering on vases, and so forth. Greek manuscripts (an-

DEVELOP-
MENT OF
GREEK
ALPHABET

Plate 63

Plates 62, 65

153

cient and medieval) number many thousands. All these documents form the basis for the studies known as Greek epigraphy
and Greek palaeography, and are of untold importance for all
branches of history – indeed, for all branches of knowledge
which have some concern, direct or indirect, with the base
of Western civilisation.

The most direct offshoots from the Greek alphabet (taking
it now as a whole) were those adapted to the languages of the
non-Hellenic peoples of western Asia Minor in the first millennium B.C.: the scripts of the Lycians, Phrygians, Pamphylians,
Lydians and Carians. The first three of these were directly
dependent on the Greek. The Lydian and Carian scripts were
strongly influenced by it, but included a considerable admix-
ture of original invention in the first case, and of Cretan, Cypriote and local forms in the second.

The Coptic alphabet was the other non-European offshoot
from the Greek and the only such offshoot used in Africa.
Twenty-five of its thirty-two letters were borrowed from the
Greek uncial writing, while seven were taken over from a
particularly cursive variety of the Egyptian demotic writing
(to express Coptic sounds which did not exist in the Greek
language).

But the most significant offshoot from the Greek alphabet
was its adaptation to the almost certainly non-Indo-European
language of the Etruscans. This event took place at a very
early period, less than two centuries after the initial adaptation
of the Semitic alphabet by the Greeks themselves; probably in
the eighth century B.C. It took place at a time when the Greek
alphabet had probably not yet diverged into its principal early

Plate 66

branches, as is shown by the Marsiliana Tablet. This unique
document, an ivory tablet of the eighth or early seventh century
B.C. found at Marsiliana d'Albegna (and now preserved in the
Archaeological Museum at Florence), was probably employed
for pedagogical purposes. Along its upper margin the entire

prototypal Etruscan alphabet of twenty-six letters is carefully engraved, running from right to left. The twenty-two Semitic letters are in their precise Semitic order followed by the four additonal Greek letters. We may, thus, assume that it was also the prototypal Greek alphabet.

Like the Semitic and early Greek alphabets the Etruscan script throughout its history was written almost consistently from right to left, though a few extant inscriptions are in *boustrophedon*.

Plates 67, 68

The Etruscan alphabet took its final, classical form at the end of the fifth century B.C., with a total of twenty letters: four vowels (*a, e, i, u*) and sixteen consonants (*g, v-digamma, z, h, th, l, m, n, p, san, r, s, t, ph, kh* and *f*). The script continued to be written in this form down into the first millennium A.D.; though with the loss of Etruscan political independence to the Romans, and the progressive replacement of Etruscan by Latin, it slowly fell into disuse. The last datable Etruscan inscriptions belong to the early first century A.D. The language lingered on for some time more; but when the Emperor Claudius began his etruscological researches in the first century A.D. it had already become something of a museum piece.

Almost no progress has been made in recent years towards the decipherment of Etruscan. The basic syntax of the language remains unknown; except for a word here and there, the few extant Etruscan inscriptions of any length remain undeciphered and undecipherable; though nearly ten thousand very short inscriptions of a religious and funerary nature can be read.

After the Etruscan script, the writing of the Messapii was the earliest European offshoot from the Greek alphabet. Originally an Illyrian people, the Messapii migrated across the Adriatic in pre-Roman times and settled in the 'heel' of Italy, in an area corresponding roughly to the modern Apulia. That the Messapian alphabet was directly adapted from the Greek

MESSAPIAN ALPHABET

is certain, though there is still no scholarly agreement as to which Greek branch or sub-branch it drew upon. The event must have taken place before the fourth century B.C. and perhaps (although the matter is uncertain) as early as the eighth century.

GOTHIC
ALPHABET

In the fourth century A.D. Wulfilas (or Ulfila), Bishop of the Visigoths, translated the Bible into the Gothic tongue ('with the exception of the Books of Kings which he omitted, because they are a mere narrative of military exploits and the Gothic tribes were especially fond of war.'). For this purpose Wulfilas invented an alphabet generally known as Gothic or Mœso-Gothic, some nineteen or twenty letters of which were taken over from the Greek uncial script, together with five or six modified signs from the Latin alphabet, and two which were either borrowed from the Runic writing or invented. Some fragments of Wulfilas's translation survive in manuscripts of the fifth and sixth centuries, the most important of which is the *Codex Argenteus*. They preserve what is by several centuries the oldest extant specimen of Teutonic speech. But this early Visigothic civilisation with its distinctive language and script had not the slightest influence on the subsequent development of Germanic culture.

SLAVONIC
ALPHABETS

More important, as derivatives from the Greek alphabet, are the two early Slavonic scripts which were invented in the ninth century A.D.: the Cyrillic and the Glagolitic.

CYRILLIC

The Cyrillic alphabet was based on the Greek uncial writing of the ninth century, and was the invention of one of the two brothers grouped under the name of St Cyril (Constantine, the more learned of the two). It comprised a total of forty-three letters, the majority of which were identical to Greek letters in shape, and in their phonetic and numerical values: but the particular richness of the Slavonic language in sounds necessitated the addition of new characters. Some of these were modifications of Greek letters; others were Greek letters connected ɔy ligatures or in simple combinations. The two Hebrew etters *ṣade* and *shin* were transformed into the Cyrillic letters for ʰe sounds *ch*, *sh* and *shch*.

The Cyrillic alphabet became, with slight modification in ᵉach case, the national script of all the Slavonic peoples who ᵻccepted their religion from Byzantium: the Bulgarians, Serbs, Russians, White Russians and Ukrainians. For a time it was ᵻlso adapted to the Rumanian language. Through the medium ɔf the Russian script, it became the writing of a number of Finno-Ugrian, Turkish, Iranian, and other peoples living ᵥithin what is today the Soviet Union.

Fig. 42, 43

In the case of the Slavonic peoples, as in the case of the Arabic alphabet and of some offshoots of the Aramaic script, ᵥe may lay down as a valid general principle that 'alphabet ɔollows religion'. The Russians, White Russians, Ukrai-ɲians, Bulgarians and Serbs accepted the Cyrillic alphabet ɔogether with the Greek Orthodox faith. Roman Catholicism ɔrought the use of the Latin alphabet to the Slovenes, Croats, Czechs, Slovaks, Poles, Wends and Lusatians. The line of demarcation for script and religion runs directly through the Slavonic lands, and 'bisects' Serbo-Croatian – a single speech ᵥritten very differently by the Greek Orthodox Serbs and the Roman Catholic Croats.

Fig. 44

The Glagolitic writing consisted of forty letters which are *externally* as unlike as could be from either the Greek or Cyrillic ᵴcripts. The characters are highly symmetrical, stylised and ɡeometric, consisting of such shapes as quadrangles, triangles ᵻnd circles, together with small tail-like appendages. No liga-ᵗures were used in writing this script.

GLAGOLITIC ALPHABET

The phonetic values of the Glagolitic symbols are, however, ᵻdentical with those of the Cyrillic alphabet. Hence there is no ᵭoubt that the two were closely related, though the precise ɲature of this relationship is still a matter for contention. It is ᵻt least possible that St Cyril invented both.

Phon. Value	Cyrill.	Russian Print Cursive	Bulgar.	Serbian	Ukrain.	Old Rum.
a	ЯА	А А	А	А	А	а
b	Б	Б Б	Б	Б	Б	Б
v	В	В В	В	В	В	В Г
g	Г	Г Г	Г	Г	Г(Т)	Г А
d	Д	Д Д	Д	Д	Д	Г А
ye	Є	Е Е	Е	Е	Е(Є)	Е Є
zh (j)	Ж Ж	Ж Ж	Ж	Ж	Ж	Ж Ж
z	З	З З	З	З	З	Ѕ Зz
i	Н	И И	И	И	З И	Н
i	І	І Ꙁ			І (Ї)	І (Ї)
y		(Й й)	(Й)	Ј	(Й)	
k	К	К Ж	К	К	К	К
l	Лл	Л л	Л	Л л ᴫ	Л	Л
m	Мм	М М	М	М	М	Л М N
n	N N	Н Ж	Н	Н ꙏ ꙑ	Н	N
o	О	О О	О	О	О	О (ω)
p	П	П П	П	П	П	П
r	Р	Р Р	Р	Р	Р	П Р С
s	С	С Є	С	С	С	С
t	Т	Т Ж	Т	Т	Т	С Т

Fig. 42 Cyrillic alphabet and its main descendants

Phon. Value	Cyrill.	Russian Print Cursive		Bulgar.	Serbian	Ukrain.	Old Rum.
ty	ħ				Ћ		
u (oo)	ɣ or	У у		У	У	У	ɣ or
f	Ф	Ф ℒ		Ф	Ф	Ф	Ф
kh	Х	Х х		Х	Х	Х	Х
ts	ч	Ц Ц		Ц	Ц	Ц	ч
ch	Ч	Ч ч		Ч	Ч	(Џ) Ч	Ч Ц
sh	ш	Ш ш		ш	ш	ш	ш
shch	ЧшТ	Щ Щ		щ		щ	Ψ
mute	Ъ	Ъ ɣ		Ъ	Ъ		Ъ
y	ʒı	Ы ы					ы
mute	ь	Ь ь		Ь	Ь	Ь	ь
ye	Ѣ	Ѣ ℒ		Ѣ			Ѣ
e	Э	Э Э					(IE)
yu	Ю	Ю ю		Ю	Ю		Ю
ya	яn	Я Я		Я	Я		ꙗ
ph	Ѳ	Ѳ Ѳ					Ѳ (ft)
y	Ѵ	Ѵ ɣ					Ѵ у
ü	Ѫ			Ж			Ѫ
iu	Ѧ ↑			IЖ			Ѧ ↑↑ ia in Ѯ Ѱ ks ps

Fig. 43 Cyrillic scripts: 1,
extant inscription, from the
Stone' A.D. 993; 2, specin
the Sviatoslav Sbornik, A.

The history of the Glagolitic script is particularly connected
with the religious history of the Slavonic peoples of the western
Balkan Peninsula. In the second half of the ninth century, the
script was introduced into the Moravian kingdom together
with the Slavonic liturgy (this was the form known as early or
'Bulgarian' Glagolitic); but with the banning of the Slavonic
liturgy by the Catholic Church it disappeared from Moravia.
It was accepted (with the Slavonic liturgy) in Bulgaria and
Croatia, and spread along the Dalmatian coast southwards into
Montenegro and westwards into Istria. It was soon 'expelled'

 КОНІБАШЕСЛОВО · НСЛОВОБѢ
ШЕѾБА · НБѢБАШЕСЛОВО ·
ТЕБѢНІКОННѾБА · БСЕТѢ ·
МЬБѢІНБЕЖНКГОНІУТОЖЕ
НЕБѢІНЖЕБѢІ · БѢТОМЬЖН

ГО ӡ̈МЬІТАРЬІ ЙГРЪ́ШЙНЙ

О ТЪЛѢСТВНЦА ؛
ТРОУПНОБАВАКМН
НЕСПѢЖТЫПРѢДННА
ГОРЬШЕКНЪНСЦѢЛѢ
ЖТЬ · ННУЬТОЖЕБО
ТАКОБѢСОМЪНПОМЫ

a Galician Evangelium, A.D.
, from the Pottara Evan-
A.D. 1561

rom the Greek Orthodox Slavonic lands by the Cyrillic
cript, but continued in use among the Catholics of the western
Balkan Peninsula, who also went on using the Slavonic litur-
y despite the disapproval of the Roman Catholic hierarchy.
Finally it was granted a special dispensation by the Church,
nd is still employed as a liturgical script in some Dalmatian
nd Montenegrin communities. It flourished briefly in the six-
eenth and seventeenth centuries, when Glagolitic printing
resses existed in Venice, Fiume, Rome, Tübingen, Siena and
lsewhere.

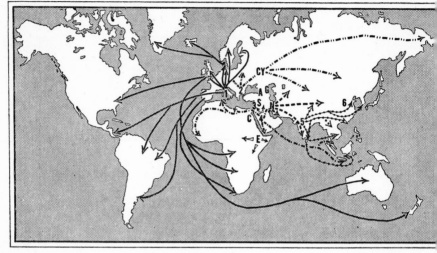

Fig. 44 'Alphabet follows Religion'
1 *Western Christianity (Latin)* (———)
2 *Eastern Christianity* ....
3 *Judaism (Hebrew)*
4 *Islam (Arabic)* (⸺·⸺·⸺)
5 *Buddhism (Buddhist scripts)* (⸺+⸺+⸺)
6 *Confucianism (Chinese script)*

Armenian **A**
Coptic **C**
Cyrillic **CY** (⸺··⸺··⸺)
Ethiopic **E**
Georgian **G**
Nestorian **N** (⸺⸺⸺)
Syriac **S**

*Fig. 45 (opposite) Runes, in all their varieties, may be regarded as the 'national' scrip
of the ancient North Germanic tribes. They probably originated in the first century B.C
or A.D. Over fifty inscriptions from what is today Denmark and Schleswig, datin
from the third to the sixth century A.D., are extant. Sixty or so Runic inscriptions hav
been found in Norway dating from the fifth to the eighth century A.D. About fift
Anglo-Saxon inscriptions have been found, including the celebrated Northumbrian cross
(A.D. 670–680), an inscription commemorating the death of King Oswiu (murdere
in A.D. 650), the scramasax, or sword-knife, found in the Thames in 1857, and th
very remarkable 'Franks Casket'. The largest number, about 2,500, have been foun
in Sweden: most of these date from the eleventh and twelfth centuries A.D.*

Phon. Value	Germanic Letters	Anglo-Saxon Letters	Scandinavian Early Signs Letters	Scandinavian Danish Late Signs Letters	Scandinavian Swed. Norw. Late Signs Letters	Dotted Letters
f	ᚠ	ᚠ ᛂ	ᚠ ᛂ ᚡ ᛦ	ᛈ	ᚡ	ᛈ
u	ᚢ ᚢ	ᚢ ᚢ	ᚢ ᚢ	ᚢ	ᚼ	ᚢ
þ	ᚦ	ᚦ ᚦ	ᚦ ᚦ ᚦ ᚦ	ᚦ	ᚦ ᚦ	ᚦ
å	ᚨ	ᚨ ᚫ	ᚨ ᚫ	ᚽ ᛂ ᚼ ᚼ	ᚽ ᚼ	ᚽ
r	ᚱ	ᚱ ᚱ	ᚱ ᚱ	ᚱ ᚱ	ᚱ	ᚱ
k	ᚲ	ᚴ ᚴ ᚴ ᚴ	ᚲ ᚲ ᚴ ᚴ ᛂ	ᚯ	ᛂ	ᚯ
g	ᚷ	ᚷ ᚷ	ᚷ			ᚯ ᚯ
w	ᚹ	ᚹ ᚹ	ᚹ ᚹ ᚹ ᚹ			
h	ᚺ ᚻ	ᚻ ᚻ	ᚻ ᚻ	ᛉ	ᛠ	ᛉ
n	ᚾ	ᚾ ᚾ ᚾ ᚾ	ᚾ ᚾ	ᚾ	ᚾ ᚾ	ᚾ
i	ᛁ	ᛁ	ᛁ	ᛁ	ᛁ	ᛁ
j	ᛜ ᛋ	ᛏ ᚦ ᚦ	ᛋ ᚦ ᛋ ᛡ ᛟ ᛜ ᛉ	ᛏ	ᚼ ᚼ ᛏ ᛏ	ᚦ
ê	ᛇ	ᛣ	ᛣ ᛋ			
p	ᚹ	ᛢ ᚻ	ᚲ ᛃ ᛒ			ᛒ ᛒ ᛘ
ř	ᛉ	ᛘ	ᛘ ᚴ	ᛙ	ᛁ	ᚪ ᚪ ᛥ
s	ᛋ ᛋ ᛋ ᛋ	ᛅ ᚾ ᚾ ᚾ ᚾ	ᛋ ᛋ ᛋ ᛋ ᛂ ᛂ	ᚾ ᚾ	ᛁ ᛁ ᛁ	ᛁ ᛈ ᛚ
t	ᛏ ᛏ	ᛏ	ᛏ	ᛏ ᛏ	ᛏ ᛏ ᛏ ᛏ	ᛏ
b	ᛒ	ᛒ ᛒ	ᛒ ᛒ ᛒ ᛒ	ᛒ ᛒ	ᚠ ᚼ ᚼ	ᛒ
e	ᛗ	ᛗ	ᛗ ᚾ ᚿ			ᛏ ᛏ
m	ᛗ	ᛗ	ᛗ ᛢ	ᛢ ᛦ	ᛏ ᛏ	ᛦ
l	ᛚ	ᛚ ᛚ	ᛚ ᛚ	ᛚ ᛚ	ᛚ ᛣ ᛉ	ᛚ
ng		ᛉ	ᛆ ᛜ ᛌ ᛆ			ᛉ
o	ᛟ	ᛟ ᛋ	ᛟ			
d	ᛞ ᛗ ᛗ	ᛗ ᛗ ᛗ	ᛗ ᛗ			ᛏ ᛏ ᛏ
a		ᛖ ᛂ				ᚦ
æ		ᛖ ᛂ				ᛁ ᛁ
y		ᛗ ᚪ ᚪ ᚪ ᚪ				ᛏ
ea		ᛉ				ᚦ ᚦ
io		ᛉ				ᛏ
c		ᛡ ᛇ ᛡ				ᚴ
g		ᚷ				

Oghams

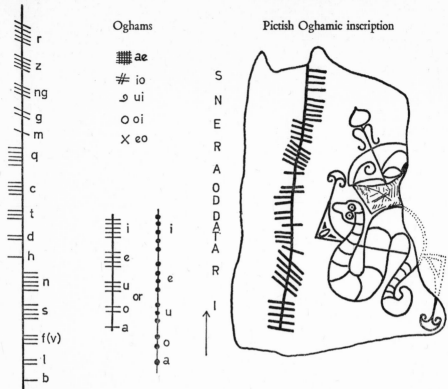

Pictish Oghamic inscription

S N E R A O D D A T A R I

Oghams

ae
io
ui
oi
eo

i
e
u
o
a

or

i
e
u
o
a

r
z
ng
g
m
q
c
t
d
h
n
s
f(v)
l
b

Fig. 46 The use of the Oghams was peculiar to the Celtic population of the British Isles. About 375 inscriptions are extant: 316 have been discovered in Ireland, chiefly in the southern counties, and 40 in Wales, particularly in the counties of Pembroke, Brecknock and Carmarthen. Only one Oghamic inscription has come to light in Cornwall, and two in Devon. One has been found at Silchester. Nearly ten have been discovered in the Isle of Man, and a few in Scotland. The inscriptions of Wales are usually bilingual (Latin-Celtic) and written in Oghamic and in Roman characters. The Irish inscriptions with one exception are in Oghamic alone.

The distribution of the Oghamic inscriptions, combined with their language and grammatical forms, point to South Wales or southern Ireland as their place of origin, and to the fourth century A.D. as the date of their origin.

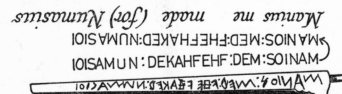

Fig. 47 Praeneste fibula

LATIN ALPHABET

The Etruscan alphabet had a number of offshoots, including
the scripts used by the Italic populations of ancient Italy (Osci,   Plates 69, 70
Umbri, Siculi, Falisci) and by such non-Italic tribes as the   RUNES AND
Piceni. The Runic writing of northern Europe, and the Ogha-   OGHAMS
mic character used by the Celts of the British Isles, may also   *Figs. 45, 46*
have been descendants of the Etruscan script through its northern (or Alpine) branch. But the most overwhelmingly important offshoot from the Etruscan writing was the Latin
alphabet.

The adaptation of the Etruscan script to the Latin language   *Fig. 47*
probably took place at some time in the seventh century B.C.
From this century we have the Præneste fibula, a gold brooch
with an inscription running from right to left which reads
manios: med: fhefhaked: numasioi, that is, *Manius me fecit Numerio*,
'Manius made me for Numasius.' The most interesting feature
of this inscription is the device of combining the letters F
(Greek *digamma*, pronounced w) and *h* to represent the Latin
sound *f*. This was one of the three Etruscan ways of representing
the same sound and indicates clearly the derivation of the Latin
alphabet from the Etruscan script. Moreover, the presence in
this inscription of the letters *d* and *o* confirms that the borrowing
took place when the Etruscan alphabet was in a very early
stage, since both these letters later fell into disuse.

From the end of the seventh or start of the sixth century B.C.   Plate 71
we have the famous *cippus* found in the Forum Romanum. On   *Fig. 48*
its four faces are the fragmentary remains of an inscription in
boustrophedon, only a few words of which can be read. Another
inscription of the sixth century, inscribed on a vase found near
the Quirinale in Rome, is still written from right to left.

Of the twenty-six Etruscan letters, the Romans adopted only
twenty-one, another three being converted into numbers. *Theta*

(☉) became Ϲ, c (100), *phi* (Φ) became ∽, M (1000) [half-*phi* became ᴅ (500)], and *chi* (\/) became ⊥, ʟ (50). A number of other changes were introduced as well: (1) the ancient Greek *zeta*, which did not represent a sound of the ancient Latin language was eventually dropped, and its place taken by a

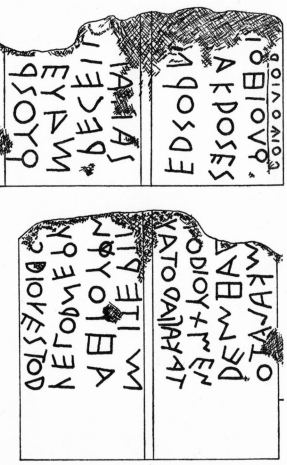

Fig. 48   The four faces of the cippus *from the Forum Romanum*

new letter for the sound *g* (C with the addition of a bar, to form G); (2) of the three Etruscan *s*-sounds, only the Greek *sigma* was retained; (3) the Etruscan form of *gamma*, which had been used by the Etruscans for the sound *k* (not differentiated by them from the sound *g*) was initially used by the Romans for both *k* and *g*, and even after the new form G had been instituted (312 B.C.), C continued to represent *g* in such familiar abbreviations as CN (for Gnæus) and C (for Gaius). Several other minor alterations were made as well.

After the conquest of Greece by the Romans in the first century B.C., the Greek symbols Y and Z were adopted as *y* and *z*, in order to facilitate the transliteration of Greek words into Latin, and were placed at the very end of the alphabet. Before this latter event had taken place, but when it had assumed its more or less final form, the Latin alphabet was as follows: A, B, C (with sound *k*), D, E, F, G, H, I, K, L, M, N, O, P, Q, P (the original shape of R, derived from the shape of the Greek letter *rho*), S, T, V, X. The addition of Y and Z brought the total number of letters in the alphabet to twenty-three.

After this time the Latin alphabet remained fundamentally unchanged. The additions attempted by Verrius Flaccus and the Emperor Claudius did not take root. The medieval additions of the letters U, W and J were actually differentiations from the existing Latin letters V and I. The history of the Latin alphabet after the first century B.C. consisted of its adaptation to various languages and the external transformation of the letters in the cursive styles.

It is a curious fact that Roman capitals, a form of writing which under the Empire was used with such unparalleled effectiveness for monumental purposes and which has become a byword for precision and grandeur, should have had so unprepossessing a childhood. For the first six centuries of its existence the Roman writing was visually unimpressive. Only

Figs. 49-51
ROMAN
CAPITALS
Plates 72, 73

in the first century B.C. do we begin to see signs of the magnificence to come. Throughout this period what we now call capitals were used for both the monumental and the literary writings: for the script which was chiseled into stone, and the script which was written on papyrus or parchment.

The specific virtues of a monumental writing have always been permanence, proportion, evenness and impressiveness. These qualities were increasingly attained and perfected by Roman capitals until they constituted a monumental writing such as the world has not seen since. Particularly was this true of what we know as the 'lapidary' capitals, one of the three principal varieties of the script. These reached their highest perfection in the *capitales quadratae* of the first and second centuries A.D. They were of equal height, carefully proportioned between parallel guiding-lines, and most of them were either square or accordingly proportioned. Some of the letters had a finishing line which we now know as a 'serif' cut perpendicularly across the ends of the strokes. A fine example of the *capitales quadratae* can be seen in the inscription on the base of Trajan's Column (A.D. 114) in Rome.

Two other varieties of Roman capitals were adapted for writing with pen and stylus: (1) the elegant book-capitals, less stiff than the lapidary writing and somewhat rounded in shape, and (2) rustic capitals, which were less carefully elaborated than the lapidary script, not so round as the book-capitals, but more easily and quickly written.

Now, whereas the virtues of a monumental writing are permanence, proportion, evenness and impressiveness, those of a script which is to be used for everyday purposes – legal, commercial and social – are of a somewhat more utilitarian order, and can usually be summed up in the single word *speed*. Hence the capital scripts were continuously modified in the writing done on surfaces other than stone, producing in the end a truly cursive Latin script. Only a very few early examples

Plates 73, 74

Fig. 50

Plate 76
Fig. 49

CURSIVE
WRITING

Plate 75

of this writing have come down to us, as a result of the more or less perishable surfaces employed: enough to indicate no more than that distinctive cursive varieties existed (e.g. those of Pompeii, and of Alburnus Major in Dacia) and that the ancient cursive script may be divided into majuscule cursive, minuscule cursive, and semi-cursive minuscule. *Fig. 49*

INTERMEDIATE STYLES

Intermediate between the monumental and cursive Latin scripts were a variety of forms: (1) lapidary and literary semi-cursive scripts, which contained a mixture of lapidary, cursive and semi-cursive characters; (2) the early semi-uncial script, which included lapidary, cursive and uncial characters; (3) the beautiful uncial style which appeared in the third century A.D., and was in the following centuries the principal book-hand; (4) the later semi-uncial style, a somewhat easier script to write, which was used from the fifth to the ninth centuries A.D. The most distinctive characteristic of the uncial letters was of course their typically rounded shape, which made this a form of writing ideally adapted for calligraphic purposes. *Fig. 50*

'NATIONAL' CURSIVE STYLES

With the final dissolution of the Roman Empire a marked change took place in the development of Latin cursive. There appeared in various places across western Europe what we must call, at the risk of mild distortion, 'national' styles of writing the cursive minuscule script. These were: *Figs. 50, 51*

(1) The Italian semi-cursive minuscule, a descendant of the Roman cursive, which was employed throughout Italy from the seventh to the ninth century. It had as its offshoots such varieties as the Lombardic (and particularly the Pavian) minuscule, the cursive styles of Amalfi, Gaeta, Naples, Lucca and Florence, the very important Ravenna script, the Papal curial style, the pre-Caroline book-hand of northern Italy (which spread into France and Germany in the eighth and ninth centuries), and the beautiful Beneventan minuscule used in southern Italy and Dalmatia, which survived all the others.

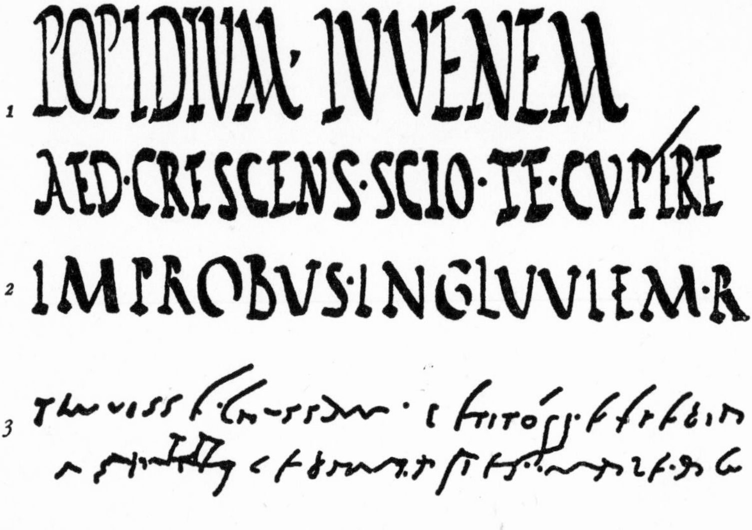

Fig. 49   Varieties of Roman capitals and cursive scripts: 1, rustic capitals from a painted wall-inscription (Popidium iuvenem aed[ilem]crescens scio te cupere), A.D. 79, Pompeii; 2, Rustic capitals from a Vergil MS of the fifth century A.D. (improbus ingluviem R[anisque]); 3, majuscule cursive from a papyrus (tenuisse caussam petitori expedia[t] (intercedant *corrected in*) ne procedant artes male ag[entibus])

(2) The Merovingian script, which was used in what we now know as France from the sixth to the eighth centuries.

(3) The Visigothic script, which was used in Spain in the eighth and ninth centuries, and which spread to Italy as well.

(4) The Germanic pre-Caroline writing, which remained highly limited in space and time (eighth-ninth centuries A.D.).

(5) The most beautiful of all the national styles: the Insular, or Anglo-Iris, hand. It developed from the semi-uncial book-hand of the early Christian missionaries to the British Isles, and not, like the Continental styles, directly from the cursive minuscule. There were two principal varieties of this script:

(a) The Irish hand, which was already in use during the

4

5

6

A.D. 51–54, Berlin; 4, majuscule cursive from a wax tablet (quinquaginta dua num
mos ob fullonicam), A.D. 57, Naples; 5, graffito in majuscule capitals (Coelius cum
Rufio et Eberiolo et Fatsto), *A.D. 79, Pompeii; 6, minuscule cursive from the* 'Papy-
rus Manni XC' (Petrus vir clarissimus comuhic chartule rex unciarum princi-
palium), *seventh century A.D., Ravenna.*

sixth century, and which some scholars contend was introduced from Gaul by St Patrick himself. It continued to be
employed throughout the Middle Ages and developed into the
modern Irish script.

Plates 77, 78

(b) The Anglo-Saxon semi-uncial style which developed
from the Irish hand in the seventh and eighth centuries, at a
time when the Roman uncial script was still predominantly
employed for the writing of manuscripts and codices. It was
employed for the writing of Latin until about A.D. 940 and for
Anglo-Saxon until after the Norman Conquest. The Anglo-
Saxon alphabet differed from the Latin chiefly in the addition
of three letters with the phonetic values *w, th* and *dh*. The so-

ABCDEFGHIK
LMNOPQRST
VWXYZ

ABCDEFGHI
KLMNOPQR

STUVWXYZ

TUBAETUOCEMAS   SICETUO
NAETCONCREGA   DERITISH

ANGELIUMDEINDEOF
FERTORIŨETDICITUR

alled *thorn* sign (ð) disappeared only with the introduction
f printing in England; the *wen* (ɣ) was replaced by the
honetically identical *w*.

The Caroline or Carolingian hand was introduced through-
ut the Frankish empire in the time of Charlemagne, though
ιe precise part which Charlemagne and Alcuin of York
layed in its creation is uncertain. There is no doubt that the
Anglo-Irish style influenced its invention to a considerable
xtent.

CAROLINE
HAND
Figs. 51-54

In the ninth and tenth centuries, the Carolingian script
ecame the principal book-hand of western Europe, and was
esponsible for the blending of majuscules and minuscules in
ιodern European scripts. The official script of the Carolingian
nperial government and (for a time) of the Chancery of the
Holy Roman Empire, it was widely employed until the twelfth
entury, and developed into localised Frankish, Italian, Ger-
ιan and English varieties. The most important of the latter
was the Winchester School hand, a particularly clear and
egible form.

Some later offshoots from the Carolingian writing were:

(1) The 'Black Letter' or 'Gothic' writing employed in
orth-western Europe, including England, until the sixteenth
entury. Here we can already see one of the characteristics of
cripts after the twelfth century: the way in which the letters
.radually assumed angular shapes of various kinds as the pen
ame to be held in a slanting position while the stroke was
ιade. German printers took over the 'Black Letter' hand as
heir principal typeface: as a result it continued to be used in
Germany as the 'national hand' after the sixteenth century and
ιnly in the past few decades has it begun to give substantial
.round before the ordinary west European typefaces.

BLACK
LETTER
Figs. 51-55

*ig. 50 opposite Latin capital and uncial book-hands: 1, elegant Roman capital
ιok-hand, fourth century A.D.; 3, uncial book-hand, eighth century; 2, uncial book-
and, fifth century; 4, late uncial book-hand.*

(2) The 'Black Letter' round hands which were used i Italy even after the introduction of the humanistic Italia cursive minuscule in the fifteenth century.

This latter form of writing was one of the most endurin products of the Renaissance in Italy. It was based on the earlie round minuscule writing which was mistakenly thought to b the script of the classical Roman period, and hence calle *antiqua*. It was initially employed only for literary productior while a secondary form – equally beautiful but not as legible was used to meet the needs of everyday life. This Renaissanc hand developed into two principal varieties: (1) the Venetia minuscule now known as *italics*, which was traditionall thought to be an imitation of the handwriting of Petrarch, an which is probably the most perfect and legible typeface eve invented; and (2) the Roman type of lettering which was per fected in northern Italy, chiefly at Venice, and used at printin presses there from the end of the fifteenth century; spreadin; thence to Holland, England, Germany, France and Spair From these two forms have developed all the typefaces ordi narily used by printers in the West today.

The legates and missionaries of the Roman Catholic Churc carried the Latin language and varieties of the Latin script t all parts of western, central, and northern Europe, confirming reinforcing and extending in this respect as in many others the influence of the defunct Roman Empire. As a result th national scripts of the majority of European peoples today ar adaptations of the Latin alphabet to Teutonic, Romance Slavonic and Finno-Ugrian languages. In many cases this ha

Fig. 51 opposite Varieties of Latin semi-uncial and minuscule styles: 1, ending of Merovingian document. A.D. 583; 2, semi-cursive from St Maximus (arum votiv solemnitate so[let qu]od remanet et suavis sapere), eighth century, Ambrosia Library, Milan; 3, the elegant semi-uncial book-hand of the Book of Kells. c. A.D. 800 4, Carolingian minuscule book-hand, ninth century; 5, black letter book-hand, fourteent century.

1.

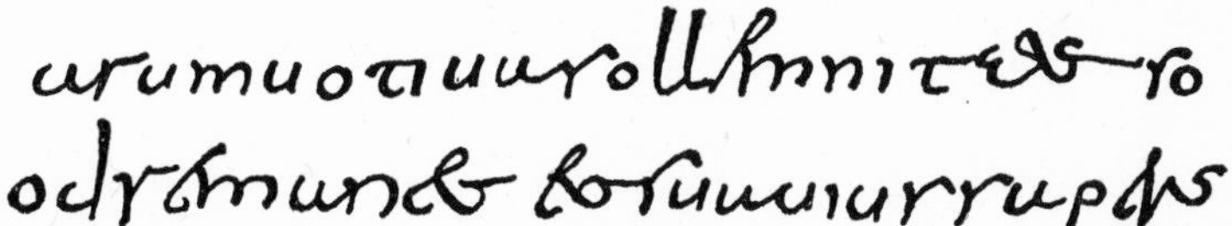

2

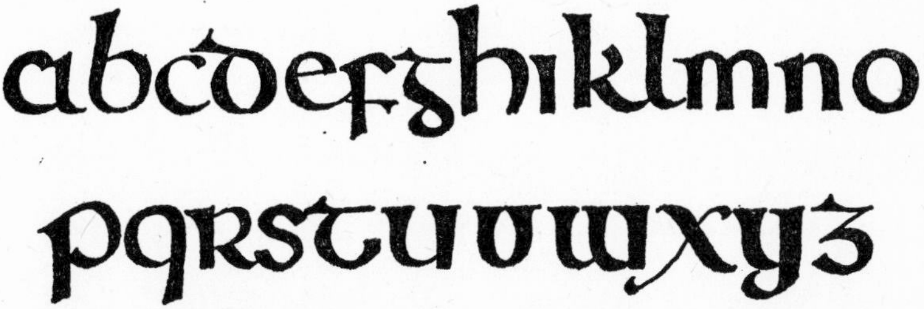

abcdefghiklmno

pqrstuvwxyz

3

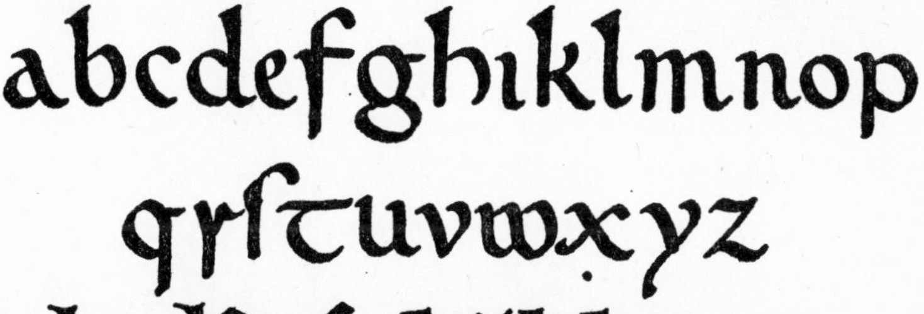

abcdefghiklmnop

qrstuvwxyz

4

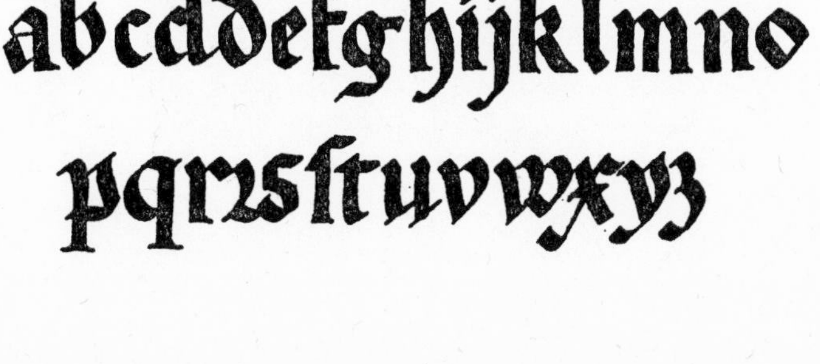

abcddefghijklmno

pqrnstuvwxyz

5

NORTH SEMITIC				GREEK				ETRUSCAN		LATIN			MODERN CAPS		
EARLY	EARLY HEBREW	MOABITE	PHOEN.	EARLY	EAST.	WEST.	CLASS.	EARLY	CLASS.	EARLY	MONUM.	CLASS.	BLACK LETTER	ITALIC	ROMAN

involved a greater or lesser number of alterations, additions, deletions and modifications, but in no case has the fundamental structure and principle of the alphabet been affected; indeed, this has remained unchanged since the origin of the Alphabet in the second millennium B.C.

Fig. 52

More recently the alphabet, in a Romanised version com‑ prising twenty‑nine letters, was introduced with singular suc‑ cess into the Turkey of Kemal Atatürk.

The activity of Christian missionaries, and the colonial ex‑ pansion of the nineteenth century, have carried it far afield into Africa and Asia, much as the Aramaic and Arabic branches of the Alphabet were once carried afield by trade, by the move‑ ment of religious conversion, and by conquest. Nor has the Alphabet in all its varieties lost anything of the dynamism which has already carried it so far: its 'conquest' may yet be incomplete we – refer, for instance, to China and Japan.

Fig. 44

Fig. 52 (opposite) Development of the Alphabet from the North‑Semitic of c. 1000 B.C. to modern capitals

APPENDIX: RECENT DECIPHERMENT OF MAYAN SCRIPT

The study of the Mayan script has been a new development in Russia since the last war, and particularly in the last ten years. In an article published in the Russian magazine *Soviet Ethnography*, 1952/No. 3, and in a book published in 1955 (*The Script of the Ancient Mayas*, in Russian and Spanish, Academy of Sciences of the USSR, Moscow, 1955), J. V. Knorozov distinguishes the following groups of the Mayan glyphs: (1) Ideograms, not many in number, the majority of the Mayan symbols being phonetic; (2) vowels, such as *a, o, e, i, u*, used mainly to represent the initial or final vocalic sound and rarely the middle vocalic sound of a word; (3) syllabic symbols representing a vowel followed by a consonant (such as *ah, ak, et*); (4) alphabetic-syllabic signs, which are sometimes employed as consonants only—at the end of a word, such as *(pa)k, (ku)tz, (ku)k*—and sometimes as syllables at the beginning of a word, such as *ka(m), tzu(l), ku(ch)*; (5) syllabic symbols, representing consonant-vowel-consonant (such as *bal, nal, thul*). His conclusions, however, have not yet been accepted by the main authorities on the subject. More recently—a year ago—S. Sobolev reported in the magazine *Soviet Union* the achievement of three young scholars (Yevreinov, Kosarev, and Ustinov) who, working under the aegis of the Siberian department of the Soviet Academy of Sciences, with the help of electronic computer techniques, have succeeded in deciphering about 40% of the Dresden and Madrid codices, or approximately 600 sentences. This research work is being carried out in Novosibirsk; the computer accomplished about one milliard operations in two full working days, but apparently for the three MSS. extant, 10 to 11 milliard operations would be required. We learn from *Atlantis*, April 1961, that Soviet scholars have stated that these MSS. will be deciphered and edited within 3-4 months. Let us hope for the best! *Chi viverà vedrà.*

General bibliography

This bibliography has been arranged in chronological sequence to show how the study of Writing has developed since the second half of the eighteenth century.

W. MASSEY, *The Origin and Progress of Letters*, London, 1763.

J. DUBOIS, *Histoire abrégée de l'écriture et moyen simple d'enseigner plus facilement la coulée*, Paris-Dijon, 1772.

T. ASTLE, *The Origin and Progress of Writing* etc., London, 1784; 2nd ed., London, 1803; another edition, London, 1876.

E. FRY, *Pantagraphia*, London, 1799.

H. J. VON KLAPROTH, *Aperçu de l'orig. des divers. écritures de l'ancien Monde*, Paris, 1832.

J. N. SILVESTRE, *Paléographie universelle* etc., Paris, 1839–41; and Sir F. Madden, *Universal Palaeography*, 2 vols., London, 1850; *Alphabet-Album*, etc., Paris, 1843.

H. N. HUMPHREYS, *The Origin and Progress of the Art of Writing*, London, 1853.

L. L. DE ROSNY, *Ecritures figuratives* etc., 2nd ed., Paris, 1870.

H. WUTTKE, *Geschichte der Schrift*, 2 vols., Leipzig, 1874-5

F. LENORMANT, *Essai sur la propagation de l'alphabet phénicien dans l'ancien monde*, 2 vols., Paris, 1872-3, 1875 (posthum.).

K. FAULMANN, *Illustrirte Geschichte der Schrift*, Vienna-Pest-Leipzig, 1880.

I. TAYLOR, *The Alphabet: an Account of the Origin and Development of Letters*, 2 vols., London, 1883; 2nd ed., London, 1899.

PH. BERGER, *Histoire de l'écriture dans l'antiquité*, Paris, 1891; 2nd ed., Paris, 1892.

F. MADAN, *Books in Manuscript* etc., London, 1893.

G. H. PUTNAM, *Books and their Makers during the Middle Ages* etc., New York and London, 1896.

E. CLODD, *The Story of the Alphabet*, London, 1900; new editions, New York, 1907, 1912, 1938; Italian translation, Turin, 1903 and 1924.

Y. B. SCHNICER, *Illustrated General History of the Scripts* (in Russian), St Petersburg, 1903.

J. E. SANDYS, *A History of Classical Scholarship* etc., Cambridge, 1903–1908.

A. MAIRE, *Materials used to write before the Invention of Printing*, Washington, 1904.

W. LOTZ, 'Die Erfindung der Schrift', *Velhag. und Klass. Monatsschr.*, 1904.

F. N. SKINNER, *Story of the Letters and Figures*, Chicago, 1905.

F. BALLHORN, *Alphabete orientalischer und okzidentalischer Sprachen*, 14th ed., Leipzig, 1906.

E. F. STRANGE, *Alphabets*, 1907.

C. DAVENPORT, *The Book: its History and Development*, London, 1907.

F. SPECHT, *Die Schrift und ihre Entwicklung*, 3rd ed., Berlin, 1909.

A. MOSSO, *The Dawn of Mediterranean Civilization*, London, 1910.

G. C. C. MASPERO, *The Dawn of Civilization*, 5th ed., London, 1910.

C. MEINHOF, 'Zur Entstehung der Schrift', *Aegyptische Zeitung*, 1911.

TH. W. DANZEL, *Die Anfänge der Schrift*, Leipzig, 1912; 2nd ed., Leipzig, 1929.

E. C. RICHARDSON, *The Beginnings of Libraries*, London and Princeton, 1914: 'Alphabet and Writing', *The International Standard Bible Encyclopedia*, Chicago, 1930.

K. WEULE, *Vom Kerbstock zum Alphabet. Urformen der Schrift,* Stuttgart, 1915. (rev. ed. *Vom Kerbstock zum Alphabet. Ersatzmittel und Vorstufen der Schrift,* Stuttgart, 1921).

A. HERTZ, 'Ein Beitrag zur Entwicklung der Schrift', *Archiv für die ges. Psychologie*, 1917; 'Les Débuts de l'écriture', *Revue Archéologique*, 1934.

E. CURTIUS, *Wort und Schrift* etc., Berlin, 1917; *Schrift und Buchmetaphorik* etc. Halle, 1942.

H. MIESES, *Die Gesetze der Schriftgeschichte*, Vienna and Leipzig, 1919.

C. F. LEHMANNHAUPT, 'Zur Herkunft des Alphabets', *Zeitschrift der Deutschen Morgenländischen Gesellschaft*, 1919.

W. A. MASON, *A History of the Art of Writing*, New York, 1920.

M. PARDO, *Storia delle scritture*, Catania, 1922.

A. HESSEL, 'Von der Schrift zum Druck', *Zeitschr. d. Deutsch. Ver. f. Buchwes. u. Schrift*, 1923.

A. MEILLET AND M. COHEN, *Les langues du monde*, Paris, 1924; 2nd ed., Paris, 1952.

REICHSDRUCKEREI, *Alphabete und Schriftzeichen*, etc., Berlin, 1924.

H. JENSEN, *Geschichte der Schrift*, Hanover, 1925; *Die Schrift in Vergangenheit und Gegenwart*, Glückstadt-Hamburg, 1935.

V. GORDON CHILDE, *The Dawn of European Civilization*, London, 1925; 6th ed., 1957.

W. OTTO, *Handbuch der Altertumswissenschaft*, Munich, 1926; *Handbuch der Archäologie*, Munich, 1939.

W. SCHMIDT, *Sprachfamilien und Sprachenkreise der Erde*, Heidelberg, 1926.

H. GRESSMANN, *Altorientalische Texte und Bilder zum Alten Testament*, 2 vols., Berlin-Leipzig, 1926–27.

WETZIG-SEEMANN, *Handbuch der Schriftarten*, Leipzig, 1926.

F. B. WIBORG and others, *Printing Ink. A History*, New York, 1926.

I. W. D. HACKH, 'The History of the Alphabet', *Scientific Monthly*, 1927.

CH. FOSSEY (ed.), various authors, *Notices sur les caractères étrangers anciens et modernes*, Paris, 1927; 2nd ed., Paris, 1948.

F. G. KENYON, *Ancient Books and Modern Discoveries*, Chicago, 1927.

(Russian title and) *Proben orientalischer Schriften der akademischen Druckerei*, Leningrad, 1928.

A. VON LE COQ, *Buried Treasures of Chinese Turkestan*, London, 1928.

H. GUPPY, 'Stepping Stones to the Art of Typography' *(Bull. of the John Rylands Library)*, Manchester, 1928; 'Human Records,' etc., *idem*, 1942.

E. DEGERING, *Die Schrift. Atlas der Schriftformen des Abendlandes* etc., Berlin, 1929.

C. FOUGÈRES, *Les premières civilisations*, Paris, 1929.

L. KÜRZ AND R. HADL, *Der naturlautliche Ursprung von Sprache und Schrift* etc., Leipzig, 1930.

A. WODRZE, 'Zum Problem der Schrift' etc., *Breslauer Dissertation*, 1930.

B. DUCATI, *La Scrittura*, Padua, 1931.

H. TENTOR, *Writing and the Origins of the Alphabet* (in Croatian), Zagreb, 1931.

M. SPRENGLING, *The Alphabet, its Rise and Development from the Sinai Inscriptions* (Excursus: A. T. Olmstead, *Excursus on the Cuneiform Alphabet of Ras Shamra* etc.), Chicago, 1931.

H. PEDERSEN, *Linguistic Science in the Nineteenth Cent.*, Cambridge (Mass.), 1931.

M. Sprengling, B. M. Parker, M. Diehl, 'The Story of Writing', American Council on Education, *Achievements of Civilisation*, I, 1932.

W. L. Graff, *Language and Languages*, New York, 1932.

M. Lejeune, 'La langage et l'écriture', *L'évolution humaine*, III, Paris, 1934.

G. F. von Ostermann and A. E. Giegengack, *Manual of Foreign Languages* etc., U.S.A. Government Printing Office, Washington, 1935; 4th ed., 1952.

A. B. Allen, *The Romance of the Alphabet*, London and New York, 1937.

D. Diringer, *L'alfabeto nella storia della civiltà*, Florence, 1937; *The Alphabet, a Key to the History of Mankind*, London and New York, 1948; 4th impr., 1952; *The Hand-produced Book*, London and New York, 1953; *The Illuminated Book*, London and New York, 1958; *The Story of the Aleph-Beth*, London, 1958; New York, 1960.

H. Bauer, 'Der Ursprung des Alphabets', *Der Alte Orient*, Leipzig, 1937

S. H. Hooke, 'The Early History of Writing', *Antiquity*, 1937; 'Recording and Writing', in Ch. Singer and others, *A History of Technology*, I, Oxford, 1954.

J. Friedrich, *Zeitschrift der deutschen morgenl. Gesellsch.*, 1937 and 1938; *Entzifferung verschollener Schriften und Sprachen*, Berlin-Göttingen-Heidelberg, 1954.

K. Sethe, *Vom Bilde zum Buchstaben* etc. (mit einem Beitrag von S. Schott), Leipzig, 1939.

C. L. T. Griffith, *The Story of Letters and Numbers*, London, 1939.

P. Carleton, *Buried Empires*, London, 1939.

W. F. Albright, *From the Stone Age to Christianity*, Baltimore, 1940 (and subsequent editions); *Archaeology and the Religion of Israel*, Baltimore, 1942 (and later ed.).

J. Tschichold, *Geschichte der Schrift in Bildern*, Basle, 1941; 3rd ed., 1951; *Schatzkammer der Schreibkunst*, Basle, 1945; *An Illustrated History of Lettering and Writing*, London, 1947; *Meisterbuch der Schrift* etc., Ravensburg, 1952.

M. Burrows, *What Mean These Stones?*, New Haven, 1941.

E. Curtius, *Schrift und Buchmetaphorik* etc., Halle, 1942.

T. Thompson, *The ABC of our Alphabet*, London and New York, 1942; new ed., 1945.

L. Lavelle, *La parole et l'écriture*, Paris, 1942.

W. J. MARTIN, *The Origin of Writing*, Jerusalem, 1942.

M. SCHLAUCH, *The Gift of Tongues*, London, 1943.

F. BODMER, *The Loom of Language*, London, 1943.

H. J. ULDALL, 'Speech and Writing', *Acta Linguistica*, 1944.

A. C. MOORHOUSE, *Writing and the Alphabet*, London, 1946; new ed. under title *The Triumph of the Alphabet. A History of Writing*, New York, 1953.

C. LOUKOTHA, *Development of Writing* (in Czech), Prague, 1946.

E. H. STURTEVANT, *An Introduction to Linguistic Science*, New Haven, 1947; new ed., 1956 and 1960.

G. CONTENAU, *Manuel d'Archéologie Orientale*, IV, Paris, 1947.

J. G. WEIGHTMAN, *On Language and Writing*, London, 1947.

A. CARLIER, *Histoire de l'écriture*, Cannes, 1947.

J. G. FÉVRIER, *Histoire de l'écriture*, Paris, 1948.

G. R. DRIVER, 'Semitic Writing' etc. *The Schweich Lectures 1944*, London, 1948; rev. ed., 1954.

L'Imprimerie Nationale de France, *Cabinet des poinçons*, Paris, 1948.

S. MORISON, *Notes on the Development of Latin Script*, Cambridge, 1949; *Aspects of Authority and Freedom in Relation to Graeco-Latin Script* etc. Lectures 1–6, privately printed, Cambridge and London, 1957.

L. HOGBEN, *From Cave Painting to Comic Strip*, London, 1949.

A. FAIRBANK, *A Book of Scripts*, Harmondsworth (Middx), 1949.

J. BOÜÜAERT, *Petite histoire de l'alphabet*, Brussels, 1949.

O. OGG, *The 26 Letters*, London, 1949; 2nd ed., 1961.

E. AND A. RELANO, *Historia gráfica de la escritura*, Madrid, 1949.

S. WEMYSS, *The Languages of the World Ancient and Modern. The Alphabets* etc., Philadelphia, 1950.

M. RAS, *Historia de la escritura y grafología*, Madrid, 1951.

I. J. GELB, *A Study of Writing. The Foundations of Grammatology*, London, 1952.

A. FINSTERER (ed.), *Hoffmanns Schriftatlas* etc., Stuttgart, 1952.

M. COHEN, *L'écriture*, Paris, 1953; *La grande invention de l'écriture et son évolution*, 3 large vols., Paris, 1958.

P. D'ANGELO, *Storia della scrittura*, Rome, 1953.

CH. HIGOUNET, *L'écriture*, Paris, 1955.

F. DENMAN, *The Shaping of our Alphabet*, New York, 1955.

R. Benz and U. Schleicher, *Kleine Geschichte der Schrift*, Heidelberg, 1956.

S. Strelcyn and others, *Writing and Book* (in Polish), Warsaw, 1958. Catalogue of Exhibition.

L. Ribeiro, *História das letras e dos algarismos*, Lisbon, 1959.

P. E. Cleator, *Lost Languages*, London, 1959.

S. A. B. Mercer, *The Origin of Writing and our Alphabet*, London, 1959.

R. S. Gilyarevskij and V. S. Grivnin, *Manual of World Languages and their Scripts* (in Russian), Moscow, 1960.

E. Doblhofer, *Voices in Stone*, London, 1961 (translation from *Zeichen und Wunder*, Vienna, 1957).

List of Acknowledgments

Every conscientious effort has been made to give due acknowledgment and full credit for borrowed material, but if through any unwitting oversight some trespass has been committed, by quoting from secondary sources, forgiveness is sought in advance, apology is freely offered, and correction promised in any subsequent editions.

Thanks are gratefully given to the following persons, institutions and publishers, for some of the illustrations used in this volume: Ankara Museum; Baghdad Museum; Dr Richard D. Barnett, Keeper of Western Asiatic Antiquities, British Museum, London; Dr Ferruccio Barreca (Cargliari, Sardinia); Brooklyn Museum; Cairo Museum; Alphabet Museum, Museum of Classical Archaeology, and University Library, Cambridge; John Chadwick, M.A. (Cambridge); H. E. Emir Maurice Chéhab, Director General of Antiquities of the Republic of Lebanon; Dr B. Ch. Chhabra, Deputy Director General, Department of Archaeology of India, Delhi; National Library of Ireland and Trinity College Library, Dublin; Royal Scottish Museum, Edinburgh; Public Relations Office, Fiji Islands; Laurenziana Library and Soprintendenza Antichità, Florence; Civic Library, Gubbio; Hazor Expedition, Jerusalem; Public Library, Leningrad; British Museum, Faber and Faber, Hutchinson's Scientific and Technical Publications, Thames and Hudson, Trustees of the late Sir Henry Wellcome, London; Glyn M. Meredith-Owens, M. A. (London); Mexico Museum; Museum of Fine Arts, Moscow; Louvre Museum, Paris; Capitolino Museum and Soprintendenza Antichità, Rome; Miss Olga Tufnell, London; Bardo Museum, Tunis; Apostolic Vatican Library and Vatican Museum; National Library, Vienna; Freer Gallery of Art, Washington.

The in-text illustrations have been drawn by Mr Anthony C. Sylvester (Cambridge) on the basis of the material preserved in the Alphabet Museum and Seminar, Cambridge.

I wish to record my gratitude to the General Editor of this series, Dr Glyn Daniel, not only for having invited me to write this book, but also for having read it in typescript and made valuable criticisms and suggestions in detail. I also tender my gratitude to Mrs Daniel for having prepared the schematic maps of this volume. A special word of thanks is due to Thames and Hudson — and particularly to Mrs Rose Bell and Mr Eric Peters who have transformed the usually burdensome technicalities of publication into a social pleasure.

Lastly, I wish to record my indebtedness to Mr James Roy, B. A., of Pembroke College, Cambridge, for his help in compiling the index.

THE PLATES

3

4

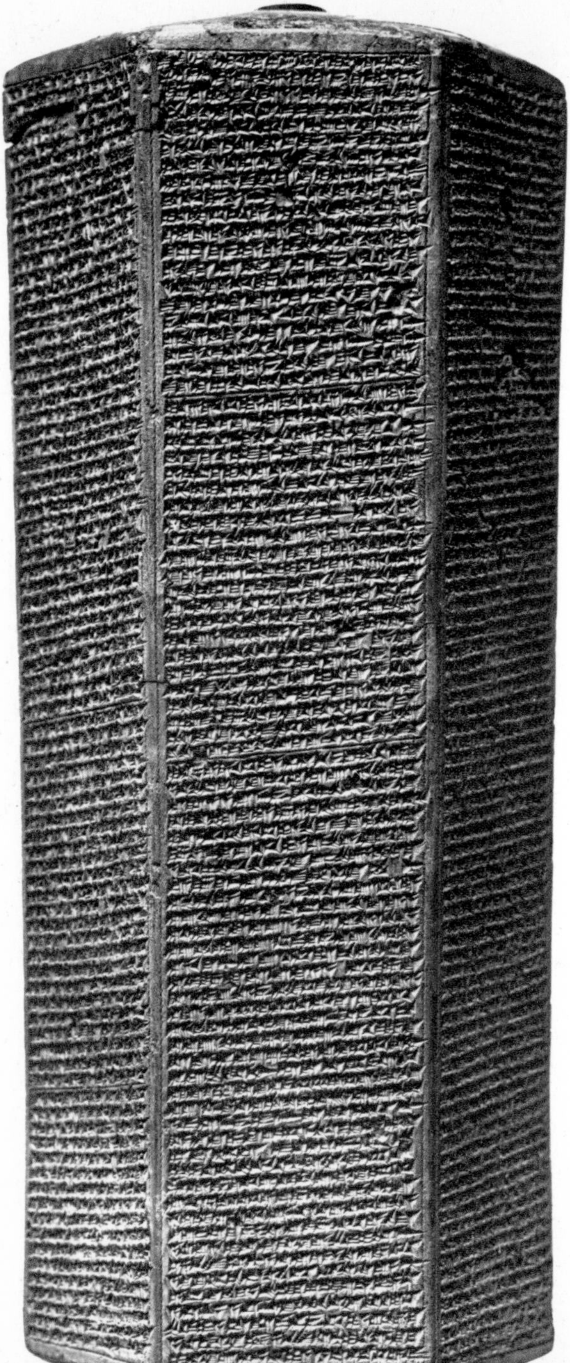

7

9

10

12

13

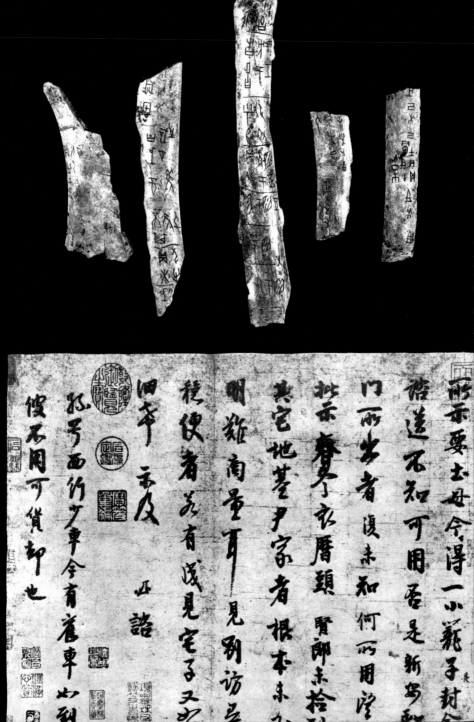

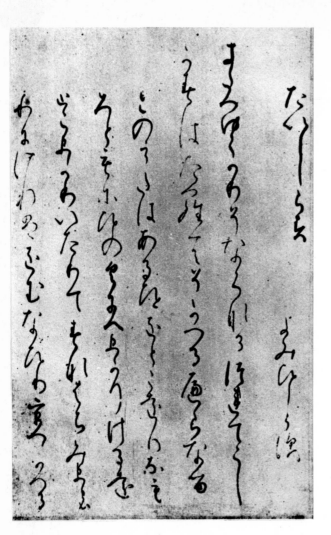

なくしらゑ　　　まけゝ浦

まきめるろなるりるほるとゝ
まはそぬてそゝつろ度るなる
このゝはあゑそゝりろふゝ
うゝをふほのゑゑよろかけま
ゝまろひたろてそれゝろまゝ
あまけわめふしなゑゐ彦ろゝ

32

33

34

36

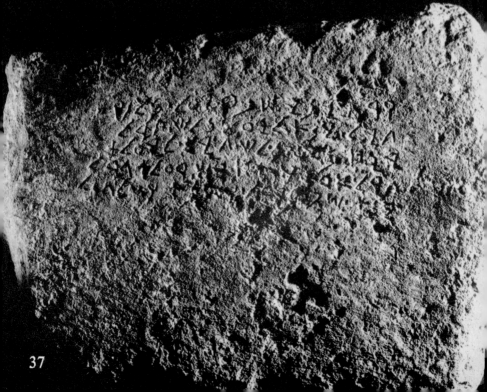

37

39

40

41

42

44

7

8

49

50

51

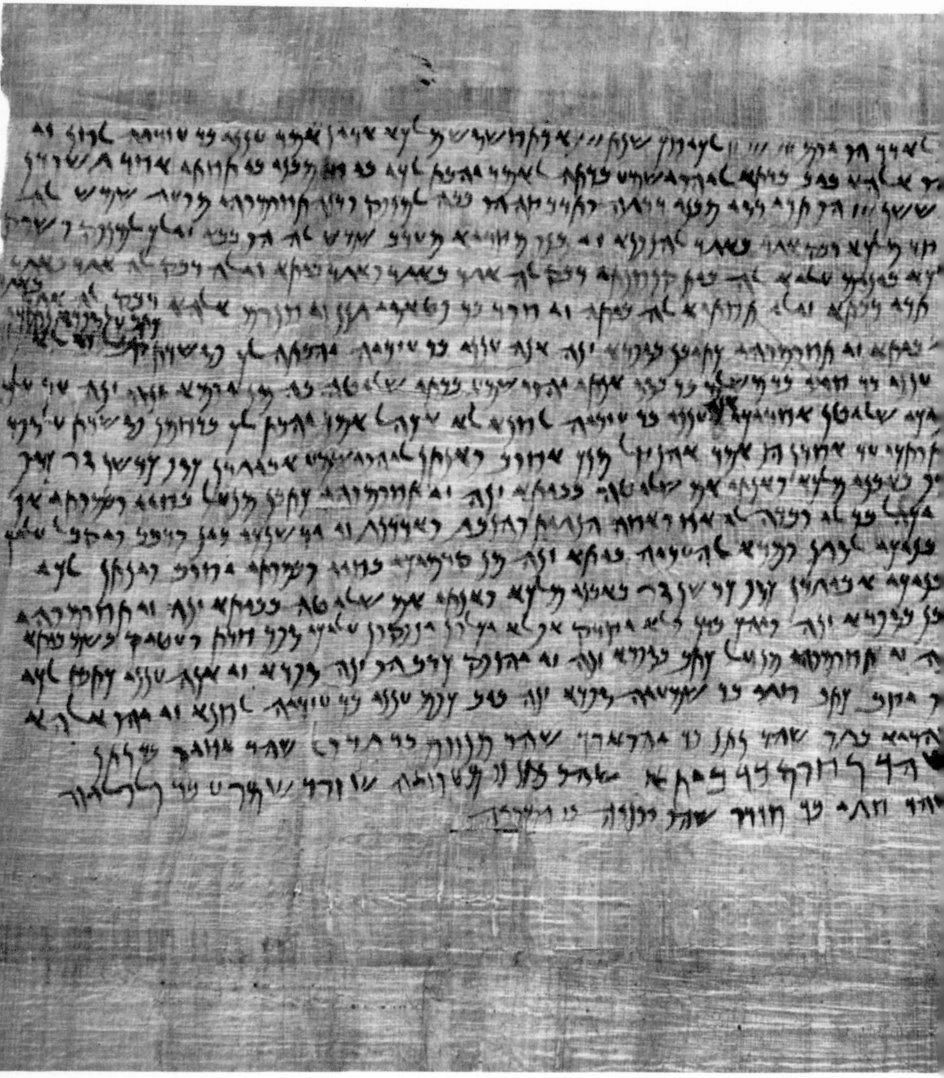

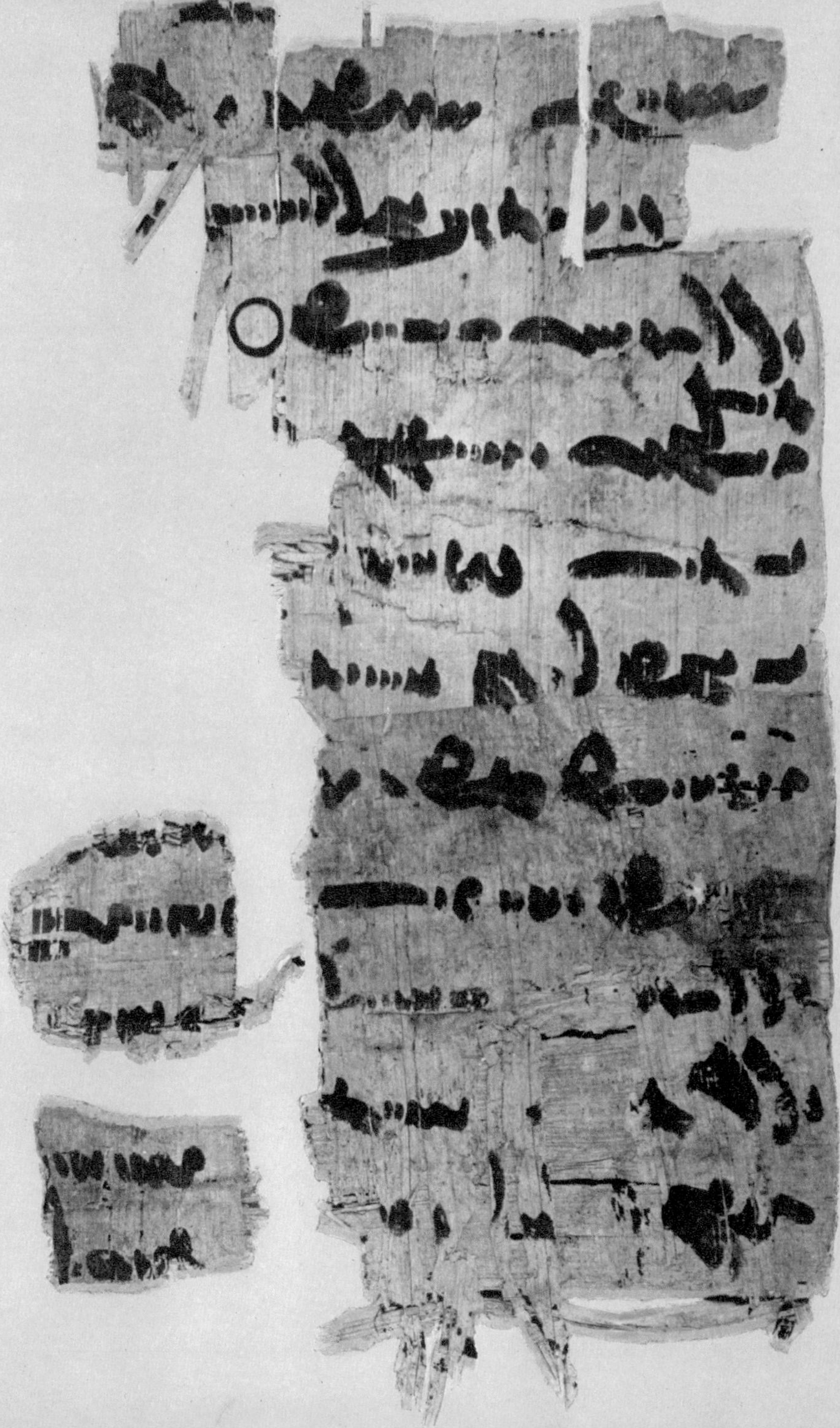

55

56

بسم الله الرحمن الرحيم

الرحمن علم القرآن خلق الإنسان علمه
البيان الشمس والقمر بحسبان والنجم والشجر
يسجدان والسماء رفعها ووضع الميزان
ألا تطغوا في الميزان وأقيموا الوزن
بالقسط ولا تخسروا الميزان والأرض وضعها
للأنام فيها فاكهة والنخل ذات الأكمام
والحب ذو العصف والريحان فبأي آلاء ربكما
تكذبان خلق الإنسان من صلصال كالفخار
وخلق الجان من مارج من نار فبأي آلاء ربكما
تكذبان رب المشرقين ورب المغربين فبأي
آلاء ربكما تكذبان مرج البحرين يلتقيان
بينهما برزخ لا يبغيان فبأي آلاء ربكما تكذبان
يخرج منهما اللؤلؤ والمرجان فبأي آلاء ربكما
تكذبان وله الجوار المنشآت في البحر كالأعلام
فبأي آلاء ربكما تكذبان كل من عليها فان
ويبقى وجه ربك ذو الجلال

كفروا يعلمون الناس السحر وما أنزل على الملكين

ببابل هاروت وماروت وما يعلمان من أحد حتى يقولا

إنما نحن فتنة فلا تكفر فيتعلمون منهما ما يفرقون به بين

المرء وزوجه وما هم بضارين به من أحد إلا بإذن الله

ويتعلمون ما يضرهم ولا ينفعهم ولقد علموا لمن

اشتراه ماله في الآخرة من خلاق ولبئس ما شروا به

أنفسهم لو كانوا يعلمون ولو أنهم آمنوا

واتقوا لمثوبة من عند الله خير لو كانوا يعلمون يا أيها

الذين آمنوا لا تقولوا راعنا وقولوا انظرنا واسمعوا

وللكافرين عذاب أليم ما يود الذين كفروا من أهل

الكتاب ولا المشركين أن ينزل عليكم من خير من ربكم

والله يختص برحمته من يشاء والله ذو الفضل العظيم

فرعین دلیل بود در مجاهدت طبعت و سیاره جزارد و سیاره جزارد و البها و البها ولکن دلیل کذ

وخاصه آنک دل بقرعت دیکر عظیم نرید و قوی تر و ما ن بعض منجل ازدانت فهم ان نرد

آن نوع بود گهدار و فتخ حرکت طبع داری نتکون ن این دلیل کنند کما الله معلوم

بسیار و طبعت رام کوبذ ماد دلیل بود در سقوط قوتت و کان ن محل از نوع بودکه

والواقع الی الوسط کوسند و این الزین ذکر ید بد او و ت کی سکون طبع داری حرکت کانب

ن دلیل بود در مجاهدت طبعت و جاک سا رطفیت و دلیل بود دصت قوت

ب ن نیضت و رام و حی کو سید دلیل و که ما در آمده است یا سرا جما یا آب

سیار یا حیز ر مطبت با دلیل بود ن او استشفا یا بسات و ذات الزیم

کمه و کراما ار الجاره الجاده نو د دلیل بود بعر و سیار که می خواهد کرد

جوان خالک و و نص موجی واحب آبذ بسیار نشو د و فوت ساط کرد دهی

موجی دو ی کرد د بازار ن بض ک رام نشاری کو نید دلیل بود برآ ماسی کرو هاب با بر

بهلو و آخرهم این ن بشاری نلی کرد ذ و دلیل بود بر سقوط قوت و نز دن نشدن بهلا د

آن بهو ک و رام ن عث کو سد یا مرن عد دلیل بود بر آ ماسی عظیم بناحیت دل

و بازداشتن از حرکت السباط و موا د سیار و حی این حال قوی تر کرد دان نسرید

آبذ کو و رام نتوی و نید و دلیل بود در هلاک ذ و نص منسبح دلیل بود بو نسنج

النور نسد که کم از ن یا ت و نما م کنم کتاب را ابو جای

تم الکتاب بعون الله وحسن توفیقه عند انسلاخ شهر ربیع الاول من سنه

ثنار و سبعین و اربع ما به و الحمد لله رب العالمین و صلواته علی سید المرسلین

محمد الصطفی و اله الطیبن الطاهرین

ՅԱՆՃԵՆԱՅԵԱԿԵ
Ն ԼՈ-ՀԵՐՈՒԵՆ :
ԵԸՆԱՅԼՀԵՆ Ա
ՊԱՐՀ ՓԵՆԱՅԵՆ
ՅԱՀԽՈՒՐՀՆՈՒԵՆ Յ :

ΕΓΛΥΨΕΝΜΕΣΙΔΗΡΟϹ
ΕΠΟΤΗΣΑΝΔΕΜΕΧΕΙΡϵϹ
ΤΕΧΝΗΓΙΠΘΟΟΜΕΝΑΙ
ΑΜΙΔΑΙΛΛΜΛΔΙΚΙϵ

63

ΟΥ ΤΗΙΣ ΔΕ ΓΕΝΟΜΕΝ
ΑΠΕΚΕΙ ΤΟ ΜΕΤ
ΤΩΝ ΔΩΔΕΚΑ +
ΕΙ ΔΩ Ϲ ΔΕ ΟΤΙ ΠΑΝ
ΤΑ ΔΕΔΩΚΕΝ ΑΥ
ΤΩΟ ΠΡ ΕΙϹ ΤΑϹ
ΧΕΙΡΑϹ ΚΟΤΙ ΑΠ·

ΘΥ ΕΞ ΗΛΘΕ ΚΑΙ
ΠΡΟϹ ΤΟΝ ΘΝ ΥΠ
ΓΕΙ· ΕΓΕΙΡΕΤΑΙ
ΕΚ ΤΟΥ ΔΕΙΠΝΟΥ
ΚΑΙ ΤΙΘΗϹΙ ΤΑ ΙΜΑ
ΤΙΑ ΚΑΙ ΛΑΒΩΝ ΛΕ
ΤΙΟΝ ΔΙΕΖΩϹ

66
67

68

74

D M S

CVCVS TOR LVATIANVS
FILIVS BONVS QVISEMPER
CARENTIBVS OBSEQVENS
VIXIT ANNIS VIII·M·VIIII·D XIII
ITEM ALIVS CVIVS LAETIANVS QVI
IDEM FIL DONVS ET OD SEQVENS
IDEM CARENTIBVS VIXIT ANNIS
M·V·M·VI·D·VI· COSVERVNT CA
TIANVS ET EVCHARIS CARENTES
FILIS DVLCISSIMIS SED NON HOC
MERENTES QVOD IS QVI SIDI SENSE
RVNT·IIII·IDVS SEPT· EXAVIDVS VNVS VIXIT IN
XT KAL OCT· ET ALIVS IN·III· KAL EASDEM

ETIAM SVA MEA PROCVILLA MVMICVLA MNATVMIANT
MAIORESQVE CADVNT ALTIS DE MONTIBVS VMBRAE

POPLA   CORYDON

O: FORMON SVM CORYDON PASTOR ARDEBAT ALEXIN
DELICIAS DOMINI NICQVID SPERARET HABEBAT
TANTVM INTER DENSAS VMBROSA CACVMINA FAGOS
ADSIDVA VENIEBAT IBI HAEC INCONDITA SOLVS

OCtessiautprimus po

ur. inordine

iuuangelium iniudia. primus scripsit cuis

uocatio adduiri expupliauis aaubus fuit

duorum ingeneratione xpi principia prae

77

78

Notes on the Plates

1, 2   Prehistoric naturalistic or schematic pictures of men and animals, crude pictures of objects, geometric patterns or other schematic carvings, on cave walls or rocks, may be considered a preliminary stage of writing. A great number of such paintings or carvings are to be found all over the world; in Europe (Spain, France, Italy, Scandinavia, and so on), Africa, Asia, America, Australia, the Pacific Islands, etc. (*See also* figs. 1–3). 1, Rock engravings near Sheik Ali River, Afghanistan. 2, Rock engravings on Yasawa Island, Fiji.

3, 4   This pictographic script, the ancestor of cuneiform writing, probably represents the earliest systematic and conscious writing anywhere in the world. (*See also* fig. 7.) 3, Sumerian tablet of the late fourth millennium B.C. The Louvre. 4, Sumerian accounting tablet of the first half of the third millennium B.C. National Museum of Iraq, Baghdad.

5–8   In the long development, lasting about two and a half millennia (from the mid third millennium B.C.), of the Akkadian cuneiform writing, two periods were outstanding. These were the early Babylonian period (practically all the extant Babylonian literature was put down in written form in that period), from the eighteenth century B.C. onwards; and the classical age of the Assyrian culture in the ninth–seventh centuries B.C. Such important inscribed monuments and written documents belonging to other periods as exist show, however, that culture, literature, science, and commerce were thriving to an extent that argues an advanced state of human society throughout the many centuries in which cuneiform writing was in use. (*See also* fig. 7). 5, Clay model of a sheep's liver inscribed with omens and magical formulae. It was employed by Babylonian priests as a guide to divination. *c.* 1700 B.C. British Museum. 6, Babylonian map of the world. Text, above, describes the campaigns of Sargon I of Agade or Akkad. The 'map' shows the ocean surrounding the world, the mountains in the North as the source of the Euphrates, the swamps at the mouth of this river, the city of Babylon, the country of Assyria, and so on. Mid twenty-fourth century B.C. British Museum. 7, Baked clay prism of the Assyrian king Sennacherib (705–681 B.C.), inscribed with an account of his invasion of Palestine and the siege of Jerusalem. British Museum. 8, The 'Sun-god Tablet', recording the restoration of the temple of Sippar by the Babylonian king Nabu-apal-iddina. *c.* 870 B.C. British Museum.

9, 10   Obverse and reverse of the Narmer Palette. This is a ceremonial slate palette of the beginning of the First Dynasty (*c.* 2900 B.C.), found in the ruins of Hiera-konpolis, the early capital of Upper Egypt. Very few documents belonging to the period of the First Dynasty have come down to us. They are regarded by some scholars as pure pictorial representation, by others as crude pictography, by others still as a transition from pictography to ideographic script, or even as the first stage of a 'transitional' script. However, they may be regarded as the *incunabula* of the Egyptian hieroglyphic writing. Cairo Museum.

11–13   From the earliest times, the ancient Egyptians had the greatest veneration for scribes, books, writing and learning. Several beautiful statuettes representing scribes (the most famous, the *Scribe accroupi*, is preserved at the Louvre, in the Salle du Scribe), bas-reliefs depicting scribes, palettes containing reeds and remains of ink, and so on, which have come down to us, are very useful for the study of how writing was done. (*See also* fig. 8). 11, Scribes and Village Elders; limestone relief from the tomb of the priest Mereruka, at Saqqara, of the period of the Sixth Dynasty, *c.* twenty-third century B.C. 12, Wooden panel carved in relief, from Saqqara; it represents Hesi-Re, a high official of the period of King Djoser. *c.* 2600 B.C. Cairo Museum. 13, Amenhotep as scribe: seated limestone statue of the Mayor and 'Chief Prophet' of Thinis. Eighteenth Dynasty (1570–1310 B.C.). Collection of the New York Historical Society in the Brooklyn Museum.

14, 15   Amongst the most interesting Egyptian MSS. extant are the recensions of the so-called *Book of the Dead*, a kind of guidebook to the underworld, containing magical formulae, glorifications, and particularly denials of guilt in various enumerated crimes and shortcomings. The earliest, the Pyramid Recension, belongs to the twenty-fifth to twenty-fourth centuries B.C. 14, Papyrus from the period of Amenhotep III (1406–1370 B.C.). Cairo Museum. 15, Late Egyptian copy of the *Book of the Dead*—Rhind Papyrus from the Roman period. Royal Scottish Museum, Edinburgh.

16 The Rosetta Stone; inscribed in hieroglyphic, demotic and Greek scripts. (*See* p. 53). British Museum.

17–21 Inscriptions in Minoan Linear A and B. The decipherment of Linear B together with the Dead Sea Scrolls (*see* p. 136) were in the fifties of the present century a focus of world interest. Ashmolean Museum, Oxford.

22 The Phaistos Disc. Notwithstanding numerous attempts at its decipherment and suggestions for its origin, the Phaistos Disc is still an enigma, and its place of origin still uncertain. Heraklion Museum; cast, Alphabet Museum, Cambridge.

23 Inscribed seals from the Indus Valley. The Indus Valley script is another puzzling problem, the more so as nothing is known about its users and their language. Indian Department of Antiquities; casts, Alphabet Museum, Cambridge.

24 Hittite hieroglyphic inscription of King Araras from Jerablus, Carchemish. This beautiful inscription, in monumental characters elaborately carved in raised relief, contrasts vividly with the late Hittite hieroglyphic inscriptions in cursive characters (exemplified by the Bulgar Dagh inscription, fig. 15). Ankara Museum.

25 Chinese inscribed oracle bones, from Hsiao-t'un, near Anyang in northern Honan. Although it is commonly (but mistakenly) believed that the origins of the Chinese script may go back to a period contemporary with that when the cuneiform and the Egyptian hieroglyphs originated, and although it is probable that Chinese writing was already in existence in the early second millennium B.C., the earliest inscriptions extant belong to the middle of that millennium. University Library, Cambridge.

26, 27   In China and Japan, calligraphy has been carried to a high pitch of perfection; indeed, it has always been regarded as the foremost of the fine arts. (*See also* fig. 16). 26, Personal letter of Li Chien∕Chung (945∕1013), a *Chin∕Shih* (i.e. possessor of the highest literary degree) and a high∕ranking Civil Servant. 27, Hiragana calligraphy by Ki No Tsurayuki (died in 946); poems from *Kokinshu*, Book 9.

28, 29   The numerous beautiful and usually well∕preserved Maya *stelae* (or huge, ver∕ tical monolithic pillars) carved all over in low relief with glyphs and figures, are exemplified by the two specimens here reproduced. 28, Mayan personified numbers and periods, from Xcalumkin Temple. Peabody Museum, Harvard University. 29, Inscription Tikal T4, L3; one of the few Mayan texts in wood. Cast in the Peabody Museum, Harvard University.

30   Dresden Codex, p. 27: ceremonies held for a new year, with Akbal as year bearer; glyphs for abundance, for west, for the death god, the new tun, drought, etc. Apart from the Dresden Codex, there are two Mayan codices extant, the Codex Peresianus in the National Library at Paris, and the Codex Tro∕ Cortesiano, preserved in Madrid.

31   Pre∕Columbian manuscript found at Ixcaquixtla, State of Puebla, Mexico. The 'Aztec' (and allied) writing is highly pictographic; indeed, more so than all the 'transitional' scripts. Practically all the symbols are more or less crude pictures.

32∕34   The Early Canaanite inscriptions may represent the earliest alphabetic writing yet discovered. (*See also* fig. 25). 32, Lachish Dagger of *c.* 1700 B.C. 33, Lachish Bowl No. 2, of the thirteenth century B.C. 34, Lachish Bowl No. 1, of the thirteenth century B.C. (*see also* fig. 26: note that the inscription is apparently upside∕down). Rockefeller Palestine Museum, Jerusalem.

35   Mesha' Stone or Moabite *Stele*. (*See also* p. 133). The Louvre; cast, Alphabet Museum, Cambridge.

36-38   The Byblos inscriptions of Akhiram (or Aḥiram), Shaphatba'al and Yekhi-
        milk (or Yeḥimilk), belonging to the eleventh century B.C. (if not earlier), may
        be regarded as a trustworthy starting-point for the history of the Alphabet. 36,
        Akhiram inscription. 37, Shaphatba'al inscription. 38, Yekhimilk inscription.
        Museum of Antiquities, Beirut.

39   Yekhawmilk (or Yeḥawmilk, Yeḥômilk) inscription of the fifth or fourth cen-
        tury B.C. Before the discovery of the Akhiram epitaph, the Yekhawmilk *stele*
        was regarded as the oldest Phoenician inscription found in Phoenicia itself.
        Museum of Antiquities, Beirut.

40   Phoenician inscription from Sardinia, found in 1838 in the locality of La
        Marmora, ancient Nora. It probably belongs to the ninth century B.C. Museum
        of Antiquities, Cagliari.

41   Fragmentary Phoenician inscription in gold. Museum of Antiquities, Cagliari.

42-45   In Sardinia, apart from the early inscriptions (cf. Plates 40, 41 and p. 132),
        several inscriptions have been discovered belonging to the Punic period, even
        to the Neo-Punic period. Several thousands of such inscriptions have been
        unearthed in the territories which belonged to the Carthaginian 'empire'. Best
        collection is that of the Bardo Museum at Tunis. 42. Neo-Punic funeral in-
        scription, from Carthage. 43, Salambo *stele*. 44, Punic *stele* from Carthage, 45,
        Neo-Punic funerary inscription from Carthage.

46   Gezer Calendar, of *c.* 1000 B.C. (i.e. belonging to the period of King Saul or
        King David). This is a small soft-stone tablet, discovered in 1908 at Gezer
        (South Palestine), on which is inscribed in Early Hebrew character, a sort of
        agricultural calendar beginning in October, or rather a list of eight months with
        the agricultural operation for each. Museum of Antiquities, Istanbul; cast,
        Alphabet Museum, Cambridge.

47   This Siloam inscription of *c.* 700 B.C., casually discovered in 1880 and now
        preserved in Instanbul, is written in the beautiful Early Hebrew monumental

style. Indeed, it is the main monumental inscription of ancient Israel, though it contains only six lines. It records the labour of those who dug the tunnel, which was probably constructed by King Hezekia (*c.* 720–692 B.C.): *see* 2 *Kings*, xx, 20; 2 *Chr.* xxxii, 3f; and 30, xxxiii, 14. Museum of Antiquities, Istanbul.

48 Early Hebrew inscription discovered in October 1956, in the excavations of the ancient site of Hazor, in Upper Galilee, and assigned to the eighth century B.C. It too is written in the Early Hebrew monumental style. Museum of Antiquities, Hebrew University, Jerusalem.

49 Early Hebrew seals, 'royal' jar-handle stamps and private seal impressions. About 150 Early Hebrew seals are still extant. But jar-handle stamps, that is, impressions of factory stamps or seals, constitute the majority of such short inscriptions. About 550 are known as the 'royal' jar-handle stamps (they contain the word *la-melekh*, 'to the king', or 'royal'); others contain private names, names of cities, etc. Nearly thirty Early Hebrew inscribed weights have also been discovered. Note the particular beauty of the top seal, of Shema', the 'servant' (i.e. the minister) of King Jeroboam (I or II).

50 *Yehud* coin. The few extant coins containing the word Yehud ('Judaea')—probably indicating the small semi-autonomous state of Judaea under Persian sovereignty—belong to the fifth or fourth century B.C. They represent a link between the pre-exilic Early Hebrew alphabet and the script on the Jewish coins from the Maccabaen age to Bar Kochba's revolt (*c.* 135 B.C.—A.D. 135).

51 Early Hebrew fragments of *Leviticus*. The *Leviticus* and other small Early Hebrew fragments, found together with the 'Dead Sea Scrolls' (*see* p. 136), are the only remains of what we consider to be the Early Hebrew book- or literary hand.

52 Modern Samaritan plate. This beautiful copper plate, written in modern Samaritan monumental style, has been presented by the Samaritan community in Holon to the President of Israel.

53 Aramaic papyrus of the fifth century B.C. from Egypt. Numerous Aramaic papyri and *ostraca* come from Egypt, among them the famous Elephantine papyri, which give us information of a religious and economic nature concern‑ ing a Jewish colony in Egypt (fifth century B.C.). Brooklyn Museum. The ear‑ liest Aramaic papyrus found in Egypt dates to 515 B.C.

54 Pahlavi papyrus (*see* pp. 148f.). Brooklyn Museum.

55, 56 Two excellent specimens of the early Kufic book style, as used for writing MSS. of the Koran. 55, Late eighth‑century Koran. National Library, Vienna, Mixt. 814, fol. 14 r. 56, Leaf from an eighth‑ to ninth‑century Koran. Freer Gallery of Art, Washington, D.C.

57, 58 Two early specimens of the very cursive Naskhi literary hand. 57, Leaf from a Koran, probably early tenth century. Private collection at Izmir. 58, Koran with Arabic glosses in Kanemba. Original at Geidam, Northern Nigeria.

59 Second earliest dated Persian MS.: A.H. 478, i.e. A.D. 1085 (the earliest being Codex Vindobonensis, *c.* 1055). Medical encyclopaedia, Bodleian Library, Oxford, MS. Pers. *c.* 37.

60 Earliest extant Syriac codex. The Rabbūla Gospels, A.D. 586. 'Syriac' was the language and script of the extensive Syriac literature, which is a Christian literature in a very special sense, since all the original documents deal exclusively with Christian subjects. Edessa, in north‑western Mesopotamia, was the first centre of Syriac‑speaking Christianity, and it became its principal focus. In fact, it was the only centre of early Christian life where the language of the Christian community was other than Greek. Edessan Syriac, after Greek the most important language in the eastern Roman empire, was used far and wide as a *lingua franca*.
The Syriac alphabet was the last important direct descendant of the Aramaic branch. The earliest datable Syriac inscription belongs to A.D. 73. The earliest document couched in Edessan Syriac and written in Estrangela character comes from Dura Europos and dates from A.D. 243. The earliest dated

Syriac MS., of A.D. 411, is probably the earliest dated codex in any language. The principal development of the Syriac scripts was encouraged by the Syriac Church, especially between the fourth and the seventh centuries. The splitting up, in the fifth century, of the Syriac alphabet into the various secondary branches (Nestorian, Jacobite, Melkite, etc.) was a direct result of the religious and political situation of eastern Christianity, which was riddled with sects, heresies, and schisms. Rabbūla Gospels, Laurentian Library, Florence, Cod. Plut. 1.56. fol. 6a.

61   Armenian thirteenth-century Gospel-book from Cilicia. Although the Armenian script, so excellently suited to the Armenian speech, was created *c.* A.D. 400, the earliest dated Armenian MSS. belong to the ninth and tenth centuries, and the majority of the MSS. belong to the twelfth and later centuries. Freer Gallery of Art, Washington D.C., Freer Gospels.

62   Earliest preserved Greek illustrated MS., attributed to 165 B.C. The earliest Greek inscription extant belongs to the late ninth or the eighth century B.C. The earliest literary work extant, written on papyrus, is attributed to the second half of the fourth century B.C. The earliest illustrated MS.—the Papyrus Letronne 1, in the Louvre, here reproduced—measures about 2 ft 8 in. in length and is perhaps a fragment of a school book.

63–65   Greek late-Classical style, and Greek uncial styles of *c.* A.D. 400 and of the eighth or tenth century. 63, Greek monumental script of the late-classical period shown in an inscription of the second century A.D. Vatican Museum; cast, Alphabet Museum, Cambridge. 64. Alexandrian Chronicle of the World, fragment 8 verso, *c.* A.D. 400. Museum of Fine Arts, Moscow. 65, Greek Lectionary of the Gospels, dated by C. R. Morey to the eighth century and by K. Weitzmann to the tenth. Public Library at Leningrad, Cod. Gr. 21.

66   Marsiliana Tablet. The earliest preserved Western ABC probably belonging to the late eighth century B.C. (*See also* p. 154f.). Archaeological Museum, Florence; cast, Alphabet Museum, Cambridge.

67, 68   Etruscan inscriptions of the third century B.C. Vatican Museum; casts, Alphabet Museum, Cambridge.

69, 70   The Etruscan alphabet had several offshoots, amongst them the Umbrian (the Umbri, whence the name of the modern Italian region of Umbria, were a people who lived in Etruria and Umbria before the Etruscan invasion) and the Picenian: the latter, a non-Italic population, perhaps of Illyrian connections, inhabited the modern central Italian region of the Marches and part of the Abruzzi, situated on the Adriatic coast. (*See also* p. 165). 69, Eugubine or Iguvine tables, containing parts of the liturgy of a sacred brotherhood of Iguvium, the modern Gubbio. This is the upper part of the fifth table, written in Umbrian script. 70, Novilara *stele* written in Picenian, belonging to *c.* 550 B.C.

71–74   Roman monumental style from the late seventh or the sixth century B.C. to the first century A.D. (*See also* figs. 47–50). 71, One of the four faces of the *cippus* from the Roman Forum, *in situ* (cast, Alphabet Museum, Cambridge). This is the oldest preserved Latin text and dates to the late seventh or early sixth century B.C. 72. Funerary inscription of Consul Lucius Mummius, the conqueror of Corinth, 146 B.C. Vatican Museum; cast, Alphabet Museum, Cambridge. 73. Inscription from the Arch of Claudius de Britannis, A.D. 51–52. Museo Capitolino, Rome; cast, Alphabet Museum, Cambridge. 74. Roman monumental script of the first century A.D.: dedication to C. Antonius Rufus, from Alexandria Troas. British Museum; cast, Alphabet Museum, Cambridge.

75   Roman cursive script of the third century A.D.: inscription of Pupus Torquatianus (*See also* fig. 49). Vatican Museum; cast, Alphabet Museum, Cambridge.

76   Roman Virgil, also known as Codex Romanus or Codex R. Cod. Vat. Lat. 3897, belonging to the fourth–sixth centuries A.D. It contains a portrait of Virgil, one of the very few extant remains of classical portrait-illustrations. The text is in rustic capitals (*see also* fig. 49).

77, 78   Excellent specimens of the Insular or Anglo-Irish hand; (77) is probably the best representative of the Irish semi-uncial or majuscule style, whereas (78) is a most famous representative of the Irish minuscule hand. 77, Book of Kells, fol. 12 recto, written *c.* A.D. 800. This is regarded by some scholars as the most beautiful book in the world. Trinity College Library, Dublin. 78, Book of Dimma (or rather, Book of Roscrea), fol. 31, recto, assigned to the eighth century A.D. Trinity College Library, Dublin.

Index